MY ALIEN NATION

A BOOK OF POETRY, AFFIRMATIONS AND REVELATIONS

JAMES MURRELL JR.
FOREWORD BY B. DWAYNE HARDIN

Printed in the United States of America. All rights reserved under International Copyright Law. This book or parts thereof may not be reproduced in any form, stored in a retrieval system or transmitted in any form by any means – electronic, mechanical, photocopy, recording or otherwise – without the express written permission of the publisher.

My Alien Nation –
2nd Edition

James Murrell, Jr.
freesoulmurrell@yahoo.com

Copyright © 2011 by James Murrell, Jr.
ISBN-13: 978-1500616267
ISBN-10: 1500616265

Cover Graphic Design by James Murrell, Jr.

Published & Edited by Cotton Works, LLC
arnettacotton@gmail.com

Acknowledgment

I acknowledge the Gift Giver, the Creator of all things, the only true and wise God, Jesus Christ. I want You to get the glory for this gift You've blessed me with. Please use it to better serve Your people and the cause of the Cross.

There are so many people whose lives have contributed, in one way or another; to the person I am today. I thank God for allowing you to be whoever you were (or are) to me in order to bring me to His glory and purpose for my life.

This acknowledgement is for my family. My parents: James and Peggy Murrell. My sisters: Michelle Bowens (Albert Bowens) and Nicole English. To my many nieces and nephews: Ashley, Sterling, Chandra, James, Jordyn, Forrest, Viqueetra and Zimarah Dickson, Lindsey, Tyler and Zoe Robinson, Jaylen Benjamin, Kyle Donovan, Kensington Dane and Kurt David English, and Bryan Wilson. To those who call me dad; Addison J. Murrell, Jacob L. Anderson and Kevin A. Miller. To my aunts and uncles, cousins and dear loved ones. Thank you all for your love and support.

Special Thanks

I want to make sure that I let certain people know how much they have meant to me in the process of writing this book and in the process of my life.

Michelle Bowens: It's no secret – you are my first and lifelong confidant. I call you for everything! I have one sister I take care of and one sister who takes care of me. Thank you for being there for me in so many ways I cannot begin to express. I love you. There is no one in this world like you; and I am eternally grateful to be your little brother.

Nicole English: Even at an early age you showed more integrity than most grown women. I'm not surprised that you've evolved into a committed, graceful, intelligent leader in your community. Thank you, little sister, for being an example to your brother of the type of woman, wife and mother that defies stereotypes and negativity. I love you.

Ashley Momanyi: What can I say kid? No uncle could be prouder to have a friend like you. Who you are to this world will never be anything less than extraordinary! The insight and intelligence you have on the weakest day could rival that of an ivy-league scholar and Nobel Peace prize winner. Thank you for being a true inspiration and an awesome niece! I love you.

Sterling Dickson: There are no words that describe the type of man you are. You are what most young men falsely claim to be, and secretly hope to become. You are honorable because you honor the men in your life like a man should. You love with your whole heart, protect and cherish your family like every parent hopes for. From one real man to the next, I love you and thank you for your example.

Lindsay Robinson: A woman with the gift of love and community. You have been gifted with a charisma unrivaled since childhood. A light so bright that in darkness, everything changes. Your future is going to be greater than your past. I've watched you grow from a sweet little girl to a wonderful mother and wife. Thank you for your support and standard of an extra ordinary woman. I love you.

Forrest Dickson: You are a man convicted with the importance of integrity toward your family and all who come in contact with you. You are a great leader because you are a great student. I admire your solid commitment toward your beliefs. Know that your family is always with you. I love you, kid.

And to my daughter, **Addison Jamese' Murrell:** Even though you are only nine years old, you have taught Daddy about love in a way no other being on earth could. I have been the most proud in life when I speak of you and the most happy in life when I am with you. The love I have inside has totally evolved beyond what I thought was humanly possible since the day you were born. I want you to know that there is no place on earth like Daddy's arms for you. I love you always, sweetheart.

- Daddy

This Book is dedicated to

my parents,
Mr. James H. Murrell, Sr. and Mrs. Peggy Murrell;
and my daughter, Addison Jamese' Murrell.
I love you eternally.

Foreword

Just imagine if David had been a dancer who suppressed his poetry because of the idiosyncratic nature attached? What if he had paid attention to what his counterparts considered "of God" and "not of God?" Imagine if he'd listened to his wife, the daughter of Saul (which means the people's choice) and followed her advice of arrogant limitation? How different would the world be?   Selah

Let's say the Psalmist Pet thought "this gift corny"
So just not use it, store it
A gift of my inner being
One that won't be seen

Locked in the corridors of my person
Held hostage to my personal thief suppression
Bound by opinion
Ruled by tradition
Governed by religion

There would not be the poetic song Psalm 23
Nor would we capture Psalm 91's safety
Psalm 51 would not have happened
'Cause Pride would have paid the stipend

We may only know about killing lions and bears
But ignorant of the wonderful deliverance of life's snares
We'd probably faint, not realizing we can't
Relenting our stand, giving in to impatient pain

Just think about it, what if
David hadn't skillfully
Penned his Psalmic Poetry?

We would know we were able to
Eat at the table prepared
In the very presence of our
Enemy who set that snare

Addendum: we wouldn't know
That to God we can speak freely
Coming boldly without inhibition
Honestly, despite religious tradition
It's just a thought . . .

In a poet whom do you seek?
One quite weak?
No, maybe a docile voice
Only able to write their choice
Choice words hidden behind pen
Without strength akin

Error my friends I say!
I see a warrior who
Wins, but expresses through pen
The pain of struggle
In rhythm to glory

One brave to kill lions – bears
But humbly trust God out of those sneaky snares
Of life's issues, simply non-resolved with only tears
Cleaned with Kleenex tissues unable to wipe away fears

This is such a one who is able to metronomically mark
Time with rhythm and rhyme
The many times
They've seen rejection
Faced defeat, yet
Learned from it the lesson

The lesson of overcoming
Stress and flesh
Fears and tears
Enemy and foe

After all, it was David who said of the Lord,
"He teaches our hands to war." Selah

That being said, I'm honored to foreword *My Alien Nation*, the poetic expressions of James Murrell's writings toward healing, victory and prophetic assurance of a fulfilled destiny. It blatantly expresses disgust, demands maturity and observes complacency as it relates to marriage, the church, women and men. It speaks from the heart with the attempt to bring healing, restoration and change.

Very few in the world are willing to transparently admit their location in life whether it was on Failure Street, Pain Avenue or Sin Alley. Few never personally journal what's on their mind, and even fewer are willing to artistically put it to pen with imaginative grace and skill, sharing with everyone their course to breakthrough and anticipation.

The people I am honored to serve as pastor are immediately taught that there's a king within them. With this in mind, demands are placed on them to pull out their royalty despite present low self-esteem, possible molestation, overwhelming rejection and lack of affirmation – no matter what. The mandate is to capture their Divine nature in overcoming their carnal tendencies.

Needless to say, the traditions of carnality don't go away without a fight of self, erroneous teachings and a repentance of mind and heart. If not, unique gifting of autoschediastical proportion will not surface to rhythmically rescue people from mental and emotional derange.

As you read or hear these brilliantly expressed writings, you will eventually find yourself in journey, only to realize that the writer has been on the same street as you. You will discover your pains weren't exclusive, that your hopes should not be aborted or that you're not alone in your thoughts.

Please know that these aren't the writings of a wimp, nor an attempt to strike out. Quite the contrary, these are the pure-hearted writings of an individual who is been broken, but not destroyed.

I guarantee you will enjoy the rhythm of poetic expression here in *My Alien Nation*. Before you're midway through this strategically written book, which provides you with a prefaced foundation of each poem, you will more than likely call a friend to share a poem or two before you encourage them to purchase their own…it's that kind of presentation.

Blessings!
B. Dwayne Hardin

Table of Contents

PREFACE xiii

01	Stormy Days	01
02	Worthy Mountain	04
03	The Day	07
04	Life	10
05	Vapor	13
06	Face N' You	15
07	Coming Back	18
08	Love's Grim Reality	22
09	Understanding	25
10	In the Way	28
11	Bouquet of Roses	31
12	One Brother's Call	35
13	Sunday Masquerade	39
14	Friendship	44
15	Gratitude.	46
16	Quest For the Pants	49
17	Block	53
18	Everyday	56
19	Shut Up!	59
20	Thorns	63
21	We Are Our Own Daddy	67
22	Out of Love	70
23	A Sober Revelation	72
24	A Bastard's Breakfast	77
25	All Day it Rained	81
26	Blue Ocean Sky	84
27	Buried Alive	87
28	Don't Ask the Children	91
29	Improbable	95
30	Jesus Did a Back Flip	98
31	My Great Father	102

32	My Parent's Porch	106
33	I Have to Dance Hard	109
34	Neopolitan	112
35	Norm	115
36	Not a Victim Anymore	118
37	On a Hillside	121
38	For Addison	123
39	King	125
40	Silenced	129
41	Speaking in Tongues	133
42	Sweet Mother of Mine	138
43	My Skin My Body	142
44	The Conscious Subconscious	144
45	The Empire	147
46	The Father's Love	150
47	The Huddle	153
48	The Sacrifice	155
49	You Took My Choice Away	157
50	The Inmate	162

My Alien Nation Preface

I want to make it clear that this journey is real. What you're about to read is not a mere compilation of rhythmic verses or stanzas cleverly organized into superficial sonnets or lyrical limericks designed to impress you. Rather, it is an accurate portrayal of the expedition of a young man who was and is gifted – yes, even anointed to define and detail intricate, complex, bewildering, astonishing and even miraculous moments in time.

While each work, in and of itself often tells its own story, the entire collection discloses the breadth and depth of the full transformation we are each designed to experience during our time on earth. James has a canny ability to capture the essence of that human emotion with words.

Whether reading in the bed or curled up in your favorite chair or couched in front of the fireplace, you will find yourself crying out loud, nodding your head, shouting amen, smiling within or calling up a friend to read a particular passage. Strap yourself in as you travel with us through *My Alien Nation*.

- Arnetta Cotton

This book has special meaning to a young man who was classified as "learning disabled" for most of his academic life. He was even encouraged not to attend college because, as he was told, "You're not smart enough." He was abused; and silently kept that secret while navigating an entire life of feeling alienated.

I'm just glad God didn't see him the way people did. After wading through belief and then disbelief, mislabeling, wrong diagnoses and lots of personal pain, he finally discovered the best of himself. Realizing he owed God both his talents and his gifts, he began on the journey to lift the once broken boy and transform him with new purpose and a love of himself so that he could represent himself in the New Alien Nation.

Introduction 01

"STORMY DAYS"

Not really like sunny days, or even days when you may be expecting a few rain clouds. No, this is a full-out stormy day. It is a day that absolutely is not going to bring you peace. It is full of nervousness and uncertainty. In parallel, it's the season when you have had your absolute fill of people's broken commitments to you. You've had your heart broken from trusting so-called loved ones who don't care as much about you as you'd like for them to. A story that's far too familiar to people who have long been treated as an afterthought, or a pawn for other's use – a victim of sorts.

Most of the people I know have developed issues behind someone who just flaked on a promise. In fact, the only way this may sound unfamiliar to you is that you are more than likely the promise breaker. I firmly believe that promise breakers do not believe they have hurt anyone…you know – no harm, no foul. They honestly think you would do well to just 'get over it'. They regularly make and then break commitments; somehow "KNOWING" that you will understand when they do not.

Since the importance of their lives and details of their existence are supposed to take precedence over everything else, you should expect broken promises from time to time; right? The problem here is that broken promises have a lifelong and lasting effect on loved ones that they may never acknowledge. I thought I would speak up for those people…

01
"STORMY DAYS"
Summer 1996

EMBEDDED TOKENS
FROM PROMISES BROKEN
COMMITTED PAINS
FROM CONSISTENT RAINS

FALLING FROM THE SKY
WITH EARNEST PURPOSE
EVERYTHING ABOUT IT
MAKES ME NERVOUS

STORMY NIGHTS
AND STORMY DAYS
THE DIMMEST LIGHTS
A CONFUSING MAZE

INTENSE FOG
AND ABUSIVE WAYS
COME TO HELP ME APPRECIATE
A BRAND NEW MORNING'S HAZE

I LIVE TO GROW
AND GROW TO LIVE
EVEN WHEN I'M EMPTY
WITH NOTHING TO GIVE

THE GLORY OF A RAINBOW
CAN NEVER BE DIMINISHED
BY THE HEARTACHE AND PAIN CAUSED
BEFORE THE RAIN IS FINISHED

STORMY NIGHTS
AND STORMY DAYS
ONLY SERVE TO BRING YOU
THE GLORY OF
"BRIGHTER RAYS!"

Introduction 02

"Worthy Mountain"

Several years back, I was invited to a town in Arkansas to spend some time with a person who I honestly thought was my friend. He seemed to empathize with me; and after learning of a series of trials I had been facing, he offered his friendship as easily as one extends a hand. He asked me to come visit in order to provide a reprieve from the emotional pressure I was experiencing due to my impending divorce and separation from my children.

Much to my surprise, the trip would eventually challenge everything I was about and everything I was struggling to become again. What I didn't know was why it would literally change everything and force me to evaluate his worth and in turn, my own. I have forgiven him for his actions, but it's not to say that I trust him anymore. Sometimes when you speculate whether or not a person is real and truthful and you embark upon a mission to expose them, you end up exposing your own propensity to lie.

This is what occurred while we raced up Pinnacle Mountain…

02
"Worthy Mountain"
02.09.09

As I stand here at the bottom of this vast, immeasurable mountain
I'm excited because I can just barely see the top
My human frailty makes me not sure I can even mount it.
Although, I feel I shall not stop.
My heart flutters in anticipation and shear excitement
As I soon learn that I will go from nervousness to near incitement.
I am confident today, that I shall look down at where I was and know I am more.
My obstacles included the height of this mountain, jagged edges, deceit and an ankle that was sore.
As I look around at the others climbing, I can see that no one is already wounded, but me.
I can hear this mountain saying to me, "If you think you can climb me, You will be great! You'll be free!"
Today, this is part of your destiny and journey. Today, this mountain is your monument of faith.
At the time, everything in me believes the adversary today is to be this vast rocky natural structure.
It was the only thing I thought I would face.
This mountain, worthy as it may be
How it blocks out the sun and mocks my attempts with its stony levels and jagged edges.
But, this day would not end with the conquering of a mountain, but that of tiny wedges.
The true adversary here turned out to be the person climbing beside me.
A contradiction to my willingness in confiding.
He will, at the end of the day, prove to me to be a liar and a deceiver.
He gnawed away at me the way a tree is destroyed by a forest beaver
How could I have trusted him? What made me such a believer?

I understand now that he was never qualified to be my friend.
I never should have given him that visa; I shouldn't have let him in.
This Worthy Mountain, which brought me home to my senses
Has given me the strength and courage to deal with these offenses.
In the name of all that is great, he only came to hate me
Every day he pretended to care and celebrate me.
He spoke just to evaluate me,
Every word now served to elevate me.
But it's ok. You know?
I've been given another day to grow.
I still have time to win.
I can still make it in
Make it in time to fully reach the top.
This mountain is worthy and now, so am I.
I've conquered another level and am higher than I.
Been given life, I've been given time
To have insight and to write more rhymes.
We came down off this little high
With the strength of our inner thighs
Now transformed was the lie in front of me
That's what I saw with my eye aside of me
Until we reached the end.

Introduction

"THE DAY"

While at work one day, Murphy's Law seemed determined to deplete my otherwise normal supply of resilience. But when I finally made it home, I had a huge revelation. After everything seemingly had gone wrong that day, I began to understand, for the first time, I should not take little things for granted.

I walked in the front door, and plopped down on the couch. Trying to find some relief, I looked out the window. A sense of calm came over me. I immediately knew that this was a transitional moment in my life just because God wanted me to notice Him.

In the rat race in which we live, it is so easy to get completely caught up in the intensity of situations (certain specific moments that appear to be altogether relevant to the fortitude of our persona), that it is almost impossible to realize the blessings of the present season, let alone possess the ability to consider the much bigger picture.

I was compelled to share how one day – one afternoon – one early evening taught me one of life's most valuable lessons.

03
"THE DAY"
11.12.98
5:50p

As I sit in my living room
looking out the door at the late afternoon hue
I'm listening to music and it,
somehow helps me understand
and know that the days are the same –
just the same as a thousand years ago
I must worship its presence.
This day is relentless in its fortitude
and it will not let me go.
It is what sustains me in my humanity
and into a peaceful conclusion.
You see, I'm depressed today –
in a certain kind of mood
that I sometimes come to when
I've fallen short of my own expectations.
In my pool of despair, I look outside.
This simple view of my day
reassures me and becomes the
stronghold of the will I had chosen this morning.
Then I know it's alright
to let the tears roll down my face.
I hold myself and cry…
I ask God for mercy and forgiveness
for the failure of today's events.
Without mercy, my life is purposeless
and dangerous in my own hands.
Now, I begin to thank God because
He's heard me and comforted me.
I feel the warmth of the sunlight over my forehead

coaxing my tears like anointing.
Once again the joy begins to flood my soul
and I am peace with myself.
I feel the music blend into my skin…
My breath grows deeper and more calm —
The day has saved me again.

Introduction 04

"LIFE"

You know, life is short! You will always have people who don't like you, or who feel they have a better plan for you than you have for yourself. Be aware, any plan they might have for you could include your ultimate failure.

In this writing, I have included some keys to having optimum life and life experiences. Sometimes we make life too hard – I know, at times, I have. And there are times when our continued response to present circumstances can thwart who we are destined to become. So much so that it requires that we back up, then rip up, like damaged carpet, that which we stood on as the foundation of our beliefs.

We all search for some form of joy in our lives. We also want to make others happy, but only as a means to be happy ourselves. I sincerely hope you learn, as I am learning, to trust yourself in order to make your life great. Come on! Let's have a great life!

04
"LIFE"
02.16.99
8:40a

For everyone else with real problems
that never seems to get corrected.
For those whom this created solvent
never seems to fix what's infected.
For those people tormented
with knowing what to do,
but can't help themselves.
For everyone whose so-called friends
won't help them out of their Hell.
Many people possess the
resilience of an entire nation;
but it doesn't help much when they know
that the evil is of their own creation.
Fathom this, that the prosperity of the wicked
still profits them nothing.
Rather, it makes them carnivores
of the wholeness they are bluffing.
Running best describes the disposition
of the decidedly damned.
Money best defines the intuitions
of those who are highly in command.
Cherish every day you have, always try to be better.
Permit yourself the right to laugh
with a sincere and earnest endeavor.
Dust off the path in which you have been chosen.
It's your life, you must begin molding moments.
Be responsible for your own peace.
Learn to love being alone.
Strive to make someone else happy

and receive the reward as your own.
God doesn't punish us as much as we do.
Learn to just let go when He is through.
This life, Baby!
And I choose to love what's ahead of me!
The only way I choose to live this life is…
More abundantly!

Introduction 05

"Vapor"

Honestly, as exciting as nature is, it can also be very, very intimidating. When a great storm arises, much fear sets in the hearts of many people because of the vast magnitude of the phenomenon. Sometimes when I see a cloud, I wonder how people can actually go through life without ever stopping to worship or wonder about its beauty or its Creator.

To me, clouds are completely pure – shrouded in mystery. They are meaningful in their own designs; and seem to be so full of purpose. If the truth be told, clouds are all we aspire to be. Yet, with all of their majesty, clouds are just a vapor that will soon dissipate into space then re-appear the next day in another place and for a different purpose.

Look up…there are clouds lingering over our heads doing exactly what they were called to do. But our hurried pace and tunneled visions cause us to ignore and take them for granted. We should all pay a little more attention to them; for they will be gone in a vapor.

05
"Vapor"
01.23.02

How can you look at the clouds
and never see more than just clouds?
Clouds are more than a ministry of sumptuous winds
They are a riddled sonnet for poets
Pure in mystery, chromatic, if you will
Seductively dancing across the sky
Arrogantly demanding one's contemplation of it;
Declaring positions of boundless power and might.
At night, the moonlight pierces through dramatic skies
with light dancing on billows of obscurity.
A setting sun may catapult the sky's evening map
into a sea of the most beautiful sienna –
full of directions and pathways to choose.
overseeing distant seas to the most golden of shores
pooling past days in a swirl of ocean and land
taking authority over any rural canvas
that seeks to command any human regard.
Vapor, come and sing away my thoughts,
Vapor, come dance away the night
Vapor....
Come bring me what will be the new morning light...
The blessed earth has presented a majestic view of who we all are:
For we are the clouds, the wind, the mighty ocean, the land and mist.
For we are merely a vapor in time.
Now, can you just look at the clouds and just see clouds?

Introduction 06

"FACE N' YOU"

For all the runners . . . whether you run away from family, responsibility, God or yourself. Even if you are not aware that you are indeed running, I want you to know that your issues will not go away simply because you don't want to deal with them. There are no vacations from life. In fact, you are not running from something created outside of you; but rather something that exists within your being.

Perhaps you, like most of us, are running from success since true success has a limited point of reference in our past and compels us into the unknown so that we can live out our purposes. It's time to stand firm in your own truth. You cannot keep running as though you are being chased. You cannot run as though running is your calling. Your issues are not dumb or irrelevant – they are real; and they have a purpose and intent that will only be made manifest by standing still. Stop running so that you can receive the prize of you. When you receive YOU then you can give YOU.

06
"FACE N' YOU"
05.99

Why are you running
When no one is chasing you?
You need to stand still and
Face what's facing you.

I'm not trying to do you any harm
It's not my will to hurt you
But, if the reality of life
Leaves you feeling alarmed
Let me be the first to alert you…

You see, this pity party you are having
Can only delay your progress
As with any part of your travel
The correct road is often the longest.

You say that you're surprised
And that you were never advised
Of how cruel this way could be.
And if what I'm telling you
Becomes a shock to you,
There's something else you should see,

You really are strong,
Stronger than you think.
You chose to ignore your strength
And prove to everyone you are weak.

If you ever get tired of running
When you get tired of blame.
You might notice something funny,
Running is just a game.

Chance is what they call it
Always running from here to there
To you, confusion is befallen
No destiny to declare.
Go back to your first love
Where you first believed,
Go back to what you thirst of,
Where your dream was conceived.

Go back and run no more
This time don't be afraid of
The way out, the opened door
Remember, you're made of more.

You can't make it go away
Or wish it wasn't there
I'm telling you there is no other way
I wouldn't even dare.

Pretend I don't know your value
And why you shouldn't run.
What you have is the power
To say that it is done.

So no matter what you encounter
No matter what you face
There's one thing it will surely amount to . . .
A very powerful thing called grace.

Introduction 07

"COMING BACK"

My wife and I were members of this particular church; and were celebrated as a wonderful young married couple within the congregation. I was involved in nearly every aspect of that ministry because I loved God and that church. I was recognized and respected as a leader. On the other hand, my wife was simply appreciated as my wife – one they perceived as loving, caring and committed.

She refused to get involved with anything; and could do nothing but find fault with the members, the leaders and even the pastor! She came to me on a regular basis crying. For some reason, she and her sister felt they were being systematically mistreated. My wife and I were struggling to communicate and our marriage was in trouble. Most people had no idea we were having problems because of the way we appeared while in church. But everything that glitters isn't gold! In order to appease my wife, we eventually left that church and went to another church. However, things grew worse between us; and we subsequently divorced.

After we divorced, I returned to the church where I thought I was loved and respected. Much to my surprise, the congregants who had once warmly embraced me and my ministry were now distant and morbidly cold. I battled incessantly with my own carnal nature. I wanted to yell and scream, "Hey y'all isn't this the same church? Your boy is bleeding, hurt and wounded! Aren't you supposed to love, understand and encourage me?" It was hard...it was very hard because I needed them so badly.

Through every service I had to constantly remind myself of who I was in Christ and of the reason why I was there in the first place. Ultimately, I couldn't stay. These were the feelings that bombarded me while sitting in church one Sunday morning.

07
"COMING BACK"
07.13.99

Lord, I'm trying to be patient.
I'm trying my best to be cool.
I'm trying to master waiting.
It's hard not to feel like a fool.
Come, sit with me, Lord
And minister to my soul.
There I know you will find me.
And in You I'll be made whole.
I still believe in Your timing
And that You remain in control.
Yet at the same time,
I know these folk ain't crazy
I know they see me sitting here.
Spiritually, it's making me raw
I'm looking for the love in here.
Could it be I've made a mistake in coming back?
Maybe I should have stayed where I was.
Every service I feel I'm under attack.
Maybe I was okay right where I was.
Where is the love that I told myself was here?
Why do I have to dance and perform
To be accepted by my peers?
This pastor has subscribed to the same
Correspondence course as old-school pastors.
The "your-Gift-Will-Make-Room-For-You
School of Dealing with Your New Bastard."

I never knew people could want to hate you
And still preach the Gospel.
Just like I didn't know they could rape you

And still call themselves Apostles.
Seriously, it's a thing that's kept me
Disappointed and perplexed —
Never knowing how I'll get treated
From one Sunday to the next.

Although my feelings are somewhat reckless
And may sound a bit hateful,
I feel compelled to tell you why, and know this . . .
Why I can still be grateful.
You see, God is consistently faithful,
More than just a little bit.
No, He reminded me I was made in His image
And to man's folly, we've created for Him, a limit.
And, at the end of the day,
God, in all of His infinite wisdom,
Is the One who really wants me anyway.
I'm coming back to Him,
Not this repressive system.
Thank God, I finally get it.
Man will hold you to his own view
And twisted side of the story —
Your faults, he will never forget.

He will make you pay and then not be sorry.
So, I am coming back.
Much stronger this time —
Not needing the approval
Of others who, like me,
Are also standing in line.
Coming back . . .
Not to others, but to Christ.
With my eyes off the people,
Making the sacrifice.

Introduction 08

"Love's Grim Reality"

This poem is about the state of emotion that comes along with a marriage that has gone wrong. Love, in this poem, is referred to as a grim awakening to the man who finds himself failing at his relationship with his wife.

The reality is that love, in and of itself, is perfect. What isn't perfect is what we have allowed love to become within us. We limit love to our past experiences, other people's opinions and advice. We limit ourselves to how much we think we can tolerate love; and eventually put a cap on trust based upon society's rules. This brief journey into my heart is mostly about my feelings after the divorce took place, "from a male perspective". It is an honest and truthful account of the mature thoughts of a man in regret.

08
"Love's Grim Reality"
07.13.99
10:15a

At some point, I fell in love with you.
To show my love and marry
Was what I was told to should do.
Looking back, I now understand
That taking your heart
Didn't mean having to take your hand.
We didn't treat each other right
As much as we thought we did,
Now that I see the light
We have a lot we must forgive.
It's true; there are two sides to every story
And, yes, there's a lot to read
Between each line of pain and glory
Beyond our wants and our needs
But who's to blame? Who's at fault?
That seems to be the retrospective task
People change, some get caught
Trying to hide the colors in their mask.
I could spend all my time hating you and pointing a finger
I figure, hating you for any length of time
Makes any hatred of me linger.
Now I can fully appreciate the experience
All this has brought me
The aspects of maturity wisdom has taught me.
So what started as grim might not be so grim at all
The hardest part is getting up after the fall
I still respect love and look for it again,
Only this time it'll be real, not pretend.

This time I will try to live my life on purpose,
Class and practicality.
And try not to recreate love's grim reality.

Introduction 09

"Understanding"

"Wisdom is the principal thing; therefore get wisdom; and with all of they getting, get understanding."
Proverbs 4:7

There's nothing like understanding to help one master his own understanding of himself. But why do some people struggle with understanding? Understanding is the final word on situations; and, it's a character adjuster like no other.

Understanding brings about ultimate truth and confidence regarding a thing or even a person. At some point, we all need understanding so that we can be real and relevant in this world. So what is the biggest challenge with understanding?

We go through most of our childhood in school gathering, learning and understanding. On new jobs, while being trained, we eagerly reach for understanding. Even in new relationships, we try hard to understand the other person, with the hope that neither one of us gets hurt.

I challenge you to find the depth of life's understanding; and in turn understand yourself – beyond your own excuses, far past other people's opinions and regardless of what you've accepted at face value. Evaluate, examine and explore who you are. Perhaps like me, once you're done pretending, all you'll desire is a better understanding of who you really are.

Understanding will bring wonderful revelation to your life. I highly recommend it to everyone.

09
"Understanding"
Hilltop Treatment Center Computer Class
11.29.99
11:10a

Strong visions seem to bombard my mind,
Some decisions make real answers so hard to find.
I can't always be there for you,
And I've gotta make it for me – oh, it's true.
Though nothing compares to the love I have for you.
You must understand the things I'm destined to do.
I'm careful to know the things you want to get,
Why must you hate the person you first met?
You see, your actions reflect your heart's real desire
It's obvious you are waiting for my desire to expire.
Self-preservation is what you choose to practice
That's what I call your my-way-or-no-way tactics
Ya' see…if you don't love me, you're free to go
Love isn't only about doing the things you know.
If I ask you to treat me nice
Why should I have to ask you twice?
I'm tripping every time I have to
Ask you to respect me
I watch you concentrate real hard not to reject me
Be an asset to me, not a liability
Be someone I want to walk with me
And not a loathsome responsibility.
If I show you that I care:
Why would you only on a dare?
Too much time has passed
And we're still on your agenda.
Too much hurt transferred
With you being a love pretender.

Strong visions seem to bombard my mind,
Some decisions make real answers so hard to find . . .
But the decision to stay with you
Somehow, anymore, is not really an issue.

Introduction 10

"In the Way"

For people who like to lie to themselves about their impact in lives of sincere, church-going people – who still do not realize it is their constant negativity and hard-hearted traditionalism that makes church unappealing.

These people spend year after year bragging, "Child, I've been in the way for most of my life . . ." When, in reality, they should be ashamed because they HAVE been in the way – "in the way" of progress, "in the way" of discipleship and "in the way" of change. Truth is, they have even been in their own way – giving place to deeply rooted fears of the unknown, of anything new and of change.

It is unfortunate, but indulging their archaic belief system and allowing them to have their own way has gotten in our way. Because they have a death grip on the past, it keeps Jesus forever dying on the Cross, God's Son perpetually relegated as Mary's little baby, the Ten Commandments as the law by which we must abide and the Old Testament as a prophecy that will never be fulfilled.

Jesus was never afraid of the future. He is not surprised by the events now taking place in the world. HE IS NOT SOMEWHERE TURNING OVER IN HIS GRAVE at what this world has become!!! In fact, He is not in the grave at all. He is alive and aware of every little thing you are afraid that He does not know about. All He wants us to do . . . is to get out of the way!

10
"In The Way"
1999

You've been in the way
For most of your life.
You don't understand
Why there's misery and strife.
You don't want to talk about it
You want to be left alone.
You would rather stay out
Than to go home.
The truth of it is that
You don't know
What you're missing.
You don't know what you lack.
You don't know
That you're tripping
Over the principles of giving back.
Been in the way
Of your own progress
Everyday seems longer
Longer than the longest.
You've been in the way
Not my way, but your own
You chose to ignore
The way which was shown
To you and all your cronies
For the sake of appearances
You all decided to stay phony.
If there wasn't more out there
You needed to become
I wouldn't bother you
I'd let you stay dumb.

The problem here
Is that you're also in our way
And we want you to move
You want to stay!
You need to choose;
You need to pray.
We have new, changed lives
And scriptures to fulfill
You have your lil' crew with gossiping lies
And new members you need to kill!
Check your doctrines
Check your beliefs
With your doctrine
Some of your patients
Should get some relief!
What is my point here?
GET OUT OF THE WAY!
Is that simple enough?
Your cover is a dead giveaway!
We all see past the fluff!
So, if you're going to live
Beneath what has been your privilege
Go do it in some dark corner
Where that seed is pointless and frivolous.
Not one more day
Not one more moment
There is a new way
You don't have to borrow it,
You can own it.

Introduction 11

"Bouquet of Roses"

I was in a tumultuous marriage back in the 1990's. It was a marriage that began as bad as it ended – too many dramatic highs and lows. At some point, we were not even on speaking terms with each other during the honeymoon! I was absolutely in love with my wife; and I felt she loved me as best she could.

Needless to say, we struggled aimlessly over everything. One of the biggest problems with this entire situation was the fact that she was so incredibly wounded by her past and childhood that the role of wife did more harm than good. I now understand that mere human love is not only defective, but is also deficient in its ability to erase a violent and sad childhood without some form of counseling.

This was written after one of our separations when she had gone to live with some friends. The friends encouraged me to try to reconcile with her in their home. It was not easy, but I gave it my best shot. I was finally able to pen this five years later . . .

11
"Bouquet of Roses"
1999

I remember the day when
I decided to reconcile with you
I felt I could still be with you
Believed we could see it all through.
After all the years of hurt and pain
It only took a few good weeks
For me to believe again
In our love and that we
Could once again be complete
This was something I believed
Our love could defeat.
So, I decided to solidify our reunion
And celebrate with communion.
From my hand and my mended heart
This bouquet of flowers was to declare
What was the beginning of a brand new start
I need you to know
That I was willing to let it all go

With trust, I released vulnerability.
And just so you'll know . . .
I was willing to let it all show
I was filled with forgiveness and humility.
I sacrificed my integrity and beliefs
For your promise
Baby, you could have had me,
If you could have just been honest.
Honest and true to yourself
No matter what the day brought
No matter what you were dealt.

The day is so vivid in my mind
When you broke my heart again
I can't leave it behind.
Though you thought it very small
I'll never forget the image of
The flowers sliding down the wall.
You'll never know what it was like
To see everything I gave just die.
Because everything I had
Anything at all
Was in this bouquet of roses
Sliding down the wall
Everything from my heart,
Everything I planned,
Every little part
Was coming from your man
I watched you cry
You watched me die.
You didn't care.
You didn't know why.
That in this bouquet of roses
When I thought I was your man
You could have been my wife
When I thought we were mending
What was our broken life.
This bouquet of roses,
Bouquet of flowers
In the sweetest moment
Everything sours.

Now, I'm watching you beg
For yet, another chance
You look at me
As though you're in some kind of trance
Taking for granted this time and this moment
I know you can't share this love we're in,
You feel you have to own it.
This bouquet of flowers extended to your heart
Has nothing to do with how we end
It's about the way we start.

It's who we are right now
And our capacity to receive
You must learn how to bow
You've gotta learn to believe.
Then and only then will you be able to accept
The next man who says he loves you
And wants you to himself.
Because this one . . . this is done, Baby
This thing has run its course
Know that this is one subject
I don't need for you to endorse
So, I loved you
Really, the best I could
But, I've had enough of you
More than I thought I would
One bouquet of roses
One bouquet of flowers
I guess everyone supposes
It's within our power
To try and make it work
And see it through to the end
But, you can't inflict this must hurt
And expect my heart to mend.
I'm really sorry we did this
I hope you never forget this.

Introduction 12

"One Brother's Call"

This poem was inspired by a conversation with a friend I hadn't seen in some years. While in Oklahoma City visiting from Kansas City, Missouri, I reconnected with this friend whom I grew up admiring as an older brother and mentor. It had been a while since we'd spoken, so we decided to catch up. I had just received some very serious revelations about my life and the direction I was to go. And, after talking with him I felt my first sense of relief from issues from the past. His understanding and advice was not wasted on deaf ears.

12
"One Brother's Call"
11.27.00
2:30p

I'm not so hard to teach,
I'm a man who is easy to reach.
My mind is open,
I'm ready learn,
Inside my heart, I yearn.
As soon as you tell me
I will know, my brother.
I will be better.
I'll start to grow from good weather.
I don't need the world right now,
I don't even need them girls right now.
Just empower the man in me
To stand on my own two feet
To be a man just like you
I must be whole. I must be complete.
You see, there's a lot of things I've gotta do
As a man, passion tends to engulf my soul
As a friend, please tell me where to go.
Hold me hostage to my own strengths.
For solitude and contentment I'll go to any length.
One conversation can change this barren life
I've waited and endured heartache every midnight.
Through it all, I've been
Much more than a conqueror
God has given me songs of joy to sing on top of it.
And for all the persecution I've had to face
Restitution finally comes for my race.
For the sake of the brotherhood
I'm trying to make this point understood;

Our sisters and children will not survive
Until our men are empowered and finally realize
What our purpose is and why we are ostracized.
What about a man is man-made
And what is natural?
What about our God is relevant
And what is practical?
Will we permit our childhood rhetoric
To lead our children?
Or should we grow up, grab a book,
Sit down and read to our children?
If we refuse to be mature and make world decisions
For our sons and daughters,
We will remain obscured and make no provisions
For our sons and daughters
What we've experienced
They're destined to repeat
Simply because the men they trusted craved defeat.
Our women have had to believe
They've needed to be fathers
Because finding ourselves
Has been too much of a bother
From time to time we all need our iron sharpened
At times we need our batteries to be jump-started.
So, thank you my brother for being available to me
And allowing me to make that call
You've helped me to be more focused, now
You've empowered me
And put this soldier back on the wall.
I'm encouraged in the most spiritual connotation
Inside my heart I want you to know
That your loyalty and care is receiving an ovation.
From one Iron Man to the next
You've empowered a warrior.
You became strength to me
Between me and my judges
Like a Supreme Court lawyer.
And I'd be remiss
Not to show my appreciation
Remiss if I didn't let you know
That ever since I visited in the fall
My life has not been the same since your call.

Maybe today is the day
You need to pick up the phone
Today is the day
You don't leave your brother alone . . .

Introduction 13

"Sunday Masquerade"

If you happen to be one of those people who have been in church all of your life, then you understand why this writing is appropriately named. The amount of energy expended to play the games, jump through the hoops and comply with all those individual, communal and denominational prejudices while navigating around each other in the house of God is absolutely exhausting!

It's often hard to stay focused. Someone once asked, "Are you a son or a servant?" Quite honestly, my answer really depended upon where I was. Oh, I know I'm a son to God, but do I have access in any of God's houses or the benefits in His house as a son if I'm subject to my brothers and sisters? If the pastor's children have access, do I have the same access?

Which father do I have to serve? God, the Bishop, the First Lady, their children? Who is the designated prodigal son? Does the pastor really understand Kingdom principles or does the Bible speak of monopoly as the reason Jesus died on the Cross and rose on the third day? The cultural acceptance of this type of religious domination relegated the congregants to mere servants who had no other choice but to fight over the spoils as well as the leftovers.

In order to control scores of well-meaning church goers, the scripture that implied, "Your gift will make room for you" was manipulated. We were groomed to believe blessings would surely come our way if we adhered to and complied with the rules and regulations as set forth by the established church. So our sanctuaries were filled with a gaggle of Believers who were subject to the tyranny of appointed officers who made us believe submission without question was the proper way to demonstrate honor and respect.

For too long, we lived through The Battle of the Churches! And you know exactly what I mean: the never-ending competition that exists between clearly drawn lines for denominational dominance. The scriptures instruct us to focus on becoming one. Our main goal and interest should be on the synchronization of our hearts and minds with God, our Father.

This writing focuses on the degradation and deterioration of true Christ-like values, which, by design, can only exist in the people of God and within the house of God.

The Fellowship of the Believers

"They devoted themselves to the Apostles' teaching and to the fellowship, to the breaking of bread and to prayer. Everyone was filled with awe, and many wonders and miraculous signs were done by the Apostles. All the Believers were together and had everything in common. Selling their possessions and goods, they gave to anyone as he had need. Every day they continued to meet together in the temple courts. They broke bread in their homes and ate together with glad and sincere hearts, praising God and enjoying the favor of all the people. And the Lord added to their number daily those who were being saved." Acts 2:42-47 NIV

We are fighting each other so vigorously that we haven't paid attention to the fact that the regal walls we have so skillfully erected over time have caused our spiritual walls to crumble. Unfortunately, the world can see our dysfunction and are laughing at the weakness in our character as well as the ineffectiveness of our witness.

13
"Sunday Masquerade"
11.30.00

Sunday morning, I try to look my best
Sometimes, I struggle, I must confess
If I act like this, which group will I fit in?
If I act like that, I suppose I'll be sure to get in!
Why must I wonder who, today,
You're giving grace to?
I'd speak to you, but I'd have to chase you.
I'd speak to the Pastor, but I'd have to race you.
Should I look for status
In this Christian Country Club?
Or should I look elsewhere
For a place representing love?
Pardon me, I digress.
This is suppose to be the house of Jesus
And we aren't here for any other reason
But to please Him.
But, every Sunday I try to compete
In what I believe is a game.
What's this got to do with me?
Tell me, is this done in Jesus' name?
When the pastor says, "Turn to your neighbor . . ."
You sigh and stretch out your little nasty hand
As though you are doing me a favor.
Every Sunday you make an appeal
For support to your committee's latest trick.
Hmmm, committee, that's funny.
What a clever name for your
Big "I", little "u" click!
Trying to prove you're more holy than all the rest
Never really dealing with your unholy mess!

This mask you wear is common placed
You don't wear it on your intentions
You wear it on your face,
We don't come from palaces,
Just common places
We're only made extraordinary
By God's amazing graces
Not one of us has arrived at 'elite status'
In the house of the Lord
Nor have we graduated from Holy Communion.
When you become a Holy Celebrity
Just make sure you have a union.
It has become so bad it stinks in God's nostrils
When He sees His children behaving this way
It's hard to believe they want to be called apostles
All I can control is the way I represent His name
And to these same people, show love all the same.
My prayer has been like this:
"So, here I am again, Lord
Feeling all bloodied and battered.
I thought I had to fight those people again, Lord!
My clothes look so tattered.
Sometimes, it's been hard for me to understand
That the battle is not mine, but Yours
I want to trust You on command
Trusting You, at the same time, has been a chore.
I'm still waiting for a breakthrough,
Still waiting for a change,
But, I'll be here next Sunday
Ready to praise Your name.
Hoping the weather will be sunny
Still hoping things aren't the same.
But, if You never change the people
If You never change their ways
Lord, I know You are a keeper
And You will always remain the same.
I now know worship extends
Past the church building
At home I need to be worship yielding!
That way wherever I go I will rise above
Whatever I see that doesn't resemble love
I'll become a vessel,

A vessel that doesn't leak.
A vessel, which in battle
Doesn't become weak.
I won't be broken
Every time they stare at me
Or even look at me crazy.
Cause every negative word
That's spoken about me
Comes out of a mask, Baby!
Dear God, I thank You
Because Your grace is till sufficient
And mercies, everyday have been new
Ain't no need in me sittin' around trippin'.
Real things, I still gotta do.
Thank You Lord for this vast revelation
Of the real life habits
Of the new 'Christian Generation.'
Thank You for Your lasting Word that says
We should treat everybody nice.
It should come from the heart and not at a price!
My job is to worship
And serve You with all of my being
Whether or not my circumstances are agreeing
Father, I commit to the investment
You've made within me
For the many gifts and talents
In which You've entrusted me
Please forgive my lack of focus and consecration
Help me take my eyes off the people
And the congregation.
So, I will try to smile and be polite
And most of all be real,
And never, ever let my praise fade . . .
And strive to never be a part of
The Sunday Masquerade."

Introduction 14

"Friendship"

I wrote this thinking about some friends of mine who stood by my side during some seriously trying times in my life. I loved them dearly. They were a couple who shared with me while my wife and I were still a couple. We spent all the time we could together – always hating to go home and leave one another. We spent the night over each other's house, cooked for each other and shared the same beliefs.

I never laughed as hard as I did when I was with them. I love them today as much as ever. I don't know how they got along without me, but I failed keep in touch with them. They were a military family and it was often months and years before we saw each other again.

The pain of our last separation was more than I was willing to process at the time. And rather than subject my heart to the emotional rollercoaster of repeatedly being temporarily cemented to the ones who will eventually have to leave again, I chose to let go and I felt they did the same.

14
"Friendship"

02.14.02

I know you must be angry
You really have every right
I didn't keep in touch with you
I didn't even write.
All I can ask is that you forgive me
And can we start from here
Because I miss you, positively?
Your friendship I still hold dear.
The years we've had some will never get.
'Made the best of love, laughter and companionship.
The many ups and downs
The many smiles and frowns
That comes with time shared
We even played Truth or Dare!
I don't want to patronize you
You're everything they say about you
This is why my heart longs to override
All of my feelings of apathy, all of my pride
And tell you that I love you
Couldn't need you more
An there's one more thing about you
I just can't ignore…
The way you feel about me
The way you show your love
When I think about it…
Your friendship is enough.

Introduction 15

"Gratitude"

Gratitude is a choice given to every man. In this case, I'm using it as a deliberate and purpose-filled decision to honor God. There are plenty of legitimate reasons in our lives to complain and be angry or even become bitter, but really, what's the use? All that stuff just compounds insult to injuries, and fosters mistrust in God – further damaging an already damaged, shattered and broken spirit. A broken spirit siphons the life out of you and has the propensity to send you to an early grave; ready or not.

I choose rather to embrace a heart of gratitude. Yes, grateful for everything – the good, the bad and the ugly. After all, the good is usually better than I ever imagined, the bad could always be worse and the ugly helps me to appreciate the simple beauties that surround me.

I'm truly grateful to be alive and with the good sense to say "Thank You."

15
"Gratitude"
03.03.02

As I stand here today
With another chance
I looked around
Not long, just at a glance
And I realize that your wrath
Has yielded to your mercy
With no aftermath
But, with uncommon courtesy.
I am a blessed man
And I will never take it back
I am a blessed man
And I'm living out the fact…
That to have favor with such a friend
Is to hold all the riches of the world in my hand
And I savor it too, until the end,
I carry your Word in my heart
Your promises spawn worship, some like art.
Sometimes, I say thank you
Many days in advance.
Most don't understand
This kind of romance.
Nevermore the old man,
No longer, the house built on sand.
I no longer need control and
I live on hallowed land.
Now Your blood is in my blood
And it washes white as snow
It cleanses me with a flood
And I am yet new and completely whole.
I am thankful to say the least

I am grateful that I have peace.
My soul is the place
Where I let Your Spirit reside
It unveils to me the face of the mysteries inside.
Until I am peculiar and gloriously uncommon
Until You have fulfilled everything
that is Your promise.
From the swells of my gratitude seas
I will bless You my Lord, while down here on my knees
With a servant's perspective
And a soldier's attitude
I say, "Thank You, Lord Jesus"
From Your son, with gratitude.

Introduction 16

"Quest for the Pants"

Far too many women out there have had to become more than they ever anticipated or even intended in their homes as well as in their lives. Some have had to try and take on the roles of the father to their children, a husband to themselves and even had to try and father their own lives. For some, this has been going on in their families for generations; grandmothers, aunts, cousins, sisters and mothers have had the same story in some families. So, now it is a modern day norm and they still are not really equipped to raise children alone who are conscious of the need for a man in the family. What do they do? Become the man? That's not possible. When a woman says she had to be 'the mother and the father' does that mean that she took on a male persona? Hopefully not. Does that mean she doesn't need a man for any of the things she's had to become? I don't believe that is a phenomenon that is natural or intended. So, when at last this woman actually gets a man in her life there is usually a struggle over who will ultimately wear the pants in the relationship or alas, the family.

These women (though it is not all their fault) have not received instructions from the type of woman who could possibly teach them how to be a wife and mother as a woman and not as a man. What's even worse is, she has never had a real conversation with a man about men or her role as a woman in the life of her man. All she's been taught about men is from other women and from a woman's perspective. Appallingly, some don't really even know the first thing about what it means to be a woman. She's never learned her real strengths and gifts given by God. This woman who is in a quest with her man over who will wear the pants is completely out of order. If she wants to dominate him and control him, what does she expect him to become? A woman? If he isn't allowed to be a man, then what is he? A child? If he hasn't learned to become a man from other men, he still has to learn...from other men. She can't teach him or verbally bash him into becoming what she feels he should already be! So, the next time a woman says, "Be a Man!" or "You're not a man!" I encourage her to check herself before she loses him. You can't insist on someone becoming something you have no idea what it takes to become. It could be that she has taken on a man's characteristics and is comparing her manhood with his?

16
"Quest for the Pants"
12.06

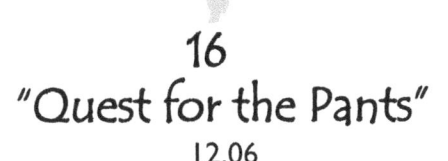

For all the years that you were in the position
You never understood your real mission
It's not that it wasn't said
You just didn't want to listen
You've had to be more than you had anticipated
High morals and family standards have been antiquated
It is only about the moment and it, how well you tell it
It's not important to live life but how well you sell it
Quest for the pants, not just yours but mine too
You have to be the boss whatever we do
Well, I'm designed and destined to wear the pants
Surely, you understand the pants are mine
I know I can't deter your quest for the pants
Just rip them off some other man's behind.
Right now you're probably be getting angry
And you are most likely deep in denial
I know you'll try to shake it off you
That dance is long out of style
(Those feelings won't go away that easy)
(And your heart is far from soft)
For generations this curse has prevailed
And all the women in your family shall be hailed...
Head.
Head and queen of any family structure
You can't understand why your men crave destruction.
Prison, abandonment or even divorce
With you there is no other course
But to give up and die
Or walk away and leave
Doesn't matter if we try
Or even beg on our knees
You are jealous

In the ugliest way
You're callous
I'm so sorry to say.
You want to be a "Strong Black Woman"
Not like the generations of women before you who were noble
You've joined a coalition of 'power pretenders'
It's not just local, it's global.
You've become unreasonable, mean and controlling
Your self-esteem is lean, unresolved and phony
Quest for the pants, not just the shirt, not just the shoes
But, you want the pants, doesn't matter whose.
You're justified, I know you believe.
But, you're wrong, madam.
It's not enough to be Eve,
You want to be Adam.
So, don't quest.
Let it go.
Do your best
To get in position
Finally, today you must know
What was always your true mission.

Introduction 17

"Block"

I, like you, am not exempt from people who want to block me from my destiny. Some people's only purpose for becoming your friend is to destroy you. They will make you believe that you cannot make progress in your life without them. Really, it's because they need to map out their plan of destruction in your life. These people will present solutions to your problems and answers to your questions. They always come posing as answers to your every need. When you have great destiny you will meet blockers and haters who are skilled at creating the perfect atmosphere conducive to your demise as though it is the sole purpose in their lives. They will marry you, pastor you, mentor you and tell you how much they love you, but it's all false. Blockers can't fool you for long, that would take too much of the focus off of them. Here's how you can spot a blocker; they have to hurry the process of getting close to you along very fast. They know it won't be long before you will really see them for who they are.

17
"Block"

We have never had shared destinies, you and I,
Even if I've included you in my life
You are not required to invest in me.
Family, best friend or even wife.
This is my life and my road to travel
Whether I'm kicking up dust or kicking up gravel.
You want what you see and what you think is potential
I don't think it's wise; don't even see it as prudential
For you to try to befriend me based upon my access
To you, I am a balloon. I know you are a cactus!
But, I intimidate you, yes, I know.
If you can't be ok with yourself
Who will imitate you, do you know?
I never asked you to be part of my fan club
And never asked for your support
I never asked you for a back rub
So why should you be a good sport?
What I'm trying to say is that 'we don't have to do this.'
When you know there's nothing to this.
I watch you squirm and bite your lip
And I know you wish I would shut up
Or just give up and quit!
How come we never talk about you and your goals?
Why is our conversation so full of holes?
You think I'm like you
Protecting your mess at any cost
But, you can't hire or even fire yourself
You aren't your mess's boss!
So, stop trying to block me
From reaching the finish line
Get your watch out and clock me

Watch me finish on time!
As long as you think you don't have value of your own....
You will believe that I need the benefit of your loan.
I don't. What God has for me, is for me.
Just know, you as well, need to learn to be free.
You've got that block thing down to a science
This isn't a friendship, it isn't even an alliance.
But, you keep on pushing it as though I'm going to give in
The problem is, it's my shoes you want to live in.
I ain't going to be able to do that
I can't be a part of your frat.
The 'So Sad Boys'
and 'The Exclusive, Elusive, Abusive Crew Shift"
'The Elite, The Special, The Original and New
The Cheaters, The Thieves, The Intimidated Dudes.
The mean girls, the haters and the chicks that are rude.
All try to block me because I see the finish line
While your goal is to stop me
Don't expect me to look behind.

Introduction 18

"Everyday"

I wrote this thought down after my becoming separated from my wife while awaiting the finalization of my divorce. I took account of what I had allowed myself to become during the relationship. I've had to be transparently honest about things of this nature for the sake of complete healing. It's truly amazing what a man finds when he gets back on track with his purpose. I will take every opportunity now to let others know that *falling in love* is possibly an admission of a certain level of failure. Falling in love is a failure to stand…in love. Who wants to fall? When you fall, you usually fall…down. Do you celebrate it? No. I've learned how important it is to choose love with your eyes wide open.

Choose to be in love. Take your time. Know exactly what it is. You don't need to be in a love stupor, it may be cute but not realistic. Completely let it go if it isn't right for who you are right now! Don't let that drunken stupor guide you into something you will regret when you sober up! How often do you sober up from love? Ladies and Gentlemen: Everyday.

18
"Everyday"
03.03.02

Everyday I back down
From what I know I should be
Everyday I'm back down
To what I said I wouldn't be.
And it's fact now,
I'm completely what I shouldn't be.
To become what you have need of
That means even if I show you I love you
Your response is what I bleed of.
 In order to be with me
You have to dominate me
If I want to be the man of us
You won't even nominate me.
My heart is at stake
And restless everyday
Navigating the weight of your quake
You can't mold me like some clay!
Why must you end me
In order to begin you?
I try to cover for you,
I try to defend you.
But the order of the day
Isn't even on the menu.
Do you want to place yourself above me
And want to become the head?
What must you think of me

Do you want me to be dead?
We've become that two-headed monster
That in all the movies gets killed!
I cannot be your sponsor
Until all your wishes are fulfilled.
Everyday I back down
With my backbone in the background!
Got my tail between my legs!
You don't want to communicate
You'd rather watch me beg!
My love, I try to demonstrate
I watch you throw a wedge!
I've had enough of you, baby
Too long I've been living on the edge.
The facts here dictate
That this really isn't about love
I'm feeling like I'm an inmate
'Cause loving you is rough.
Constantly fighting your strength
And I still don't know why you're strong.
You will go to any length
To make a grown man wrong.
Because otherwise, your legacy
Has no meaning
And it would have to end here.
If you could embrace your own destiny
And the reason for your being
Everything else would become clear.
You are never truly winning
Then when you measure your strength with a man
You will have to go back to the beginning...
When man was created from the sand
And pull Eve from the dirt
Then she, too, would be a man.

Introduction 19

"Shut Up!"

There comes a time in a man's life when he, Christian or not, sweet or not, careful or not, has to be as assertive as he knows how. Then there's that other time when he just needs you to 'Shut Up!' There are no sweet ways of saying it, no kind, thoughtful, image protecting, feelings protecting way to say it. Just shut up!

You know, I've often been accused of being mean (Yeah, I know, right? "You, James?" Yes, me!), but I am not exempt from having enough of those people who feel it's alright to abuse you. Especially if you are a nice guy who has a tendency to meet women who feel as if you are supposed to take all of the rage and misunderstandings all the rest of the men in her life inflicted upon her without regard to its impact. Consequently, she has absolutely no respect for its potential harm in your life.

I know Christian men who secretly call their wives 'Bitch' and say they want her to 'Shut The F**** Up!' The rage here in relationships is easily transferred. There is no other point. So, where do we begin to heal? Who takes the first step? Who takes the blame? Should someone take the blame? Is this even about blame? We have to stop pretending that there's some type of workable resolution within the male and female relationship today by saying incredibly mean and hurtful things to each other. Some of the things said to men are things like, "All you men are dogs!" and "Just be a man about it!", "He's a dead-beat dad!" "Men are intimidated by me." Or to women, "She's a Bitch!", "It's a man's world!", "You must be on your period." People, there is mutual responsibility here!

Men have no idea what it means to be a woman and women have no idea what it takes to be a man. Rhetoric isn't going to help us begin to challenge some of the fantastically wrong thinking we both have endured hearing for generations. The truth is; if he can't hit you, then don't hit him! If he can't talk to you like that, then stop talking to him like that! You cannot have a long list of 'must-haves' that you don't measure up to yourself. You cannot bully anyone into the love you truly need. You can't control a man with your sharp tongue, your attitude or your sex! Men aren't bearded women in disguise! In reality, men protect their hearts the way women protect their bodies. If he confides in you in a sweet moment from the treasures of his heart, don't turn around and use his secret against him in a fit of rage in order to win the argument!!! Because where he'll go to hide from you is a place you will NEVER, ever find him again!

What EVER you've been taught in your childhood will UNDOUBTEDLY manifest in your relationships! But, remember, so will what EVER he has been taught. Relationships work best with plenty of grace and mercy.

In the interim, in a tense moment this is what your man would like you to know...

19
"Shut Up!"
02.11.02
10:17a

I'm not prolific at lying to you, I must confess
And I'm not even that clever
At getting underneath your dress.
I know most guys want you to trust in them. Hmm, that's odd....
I thought you were supposed to put your trust in God.
You see, I'd like to think that I'm an intelligent man
And mysteries of the world are at my disposal
But, there's one thing I don't understand
Why would you interpret sex as a marriage proposal?
I can't save you, nor can I heal you with my love
I know you'd be a slave to me, and you'd still try to call it love.
Thinking that your femininity will knock a brother to his knees…..
Please!
That's right, baby; I ain't 'whipped' today
No, you haven't put it on me
Yeah, baby! I'm rationing the dick today
Too much about you is phony!
Sometimes you say the stupidest things
Like how much money yo' little job brings
You try to compare it to mine and make me feel jealous
You always believe it will embarrass me in front of the fellas.
Today, I've got news for you and today I serve you notice…
I don't mean to confuse you, we just gon' change your focus!
You see, …
I'm taking my manhood back from you
I'm getting back my backbone like déjà!
Get off my jock and get out of my britches
You've been on my nuts like inmates to snitches.
Go wipe my smile off your face

My happiness, you never knew how to taste!
How you gone keep trippin' and still try to keep me
Baby, I will walk out and keep livin, believe me!
"You are not man enough for me!" remember that?
Some guys would have buckled under that attack!
See, baby, you can't live on clichés and popular culture
You're not like a real woman,
No, you're more like a vulture!
But, you know I ain't trying to hurt you
It's alright to let this poem work you!
Take some good advice on how to live your best life.
You should be prepared to be a good man's wife!
You're wasting time cultivating a hood rat mentality
You should have been practicing good love, common sense and rehearsing sensuality.
I wanted you and needed you, no doubt.
But, if you must keep that funky attitude
Keep walking until, of my life, you're out.
Please shut up. You aren't right all the time.
Sometimes the feelings you are stepping on
Aren't other peoples, they're mine.
So, I had to drop you this line
Before I ran out of time…
I don't mean to confuse…
But, freedom is what I choose.
Instead of letting these words make you swell up…
Go Somewhere and Just Shut the Hell Up!!!

Introduction 20

"Thorns"

The act of apathy, being indifferent, becoming nonchalant... these are some of the terms that **may unfairly** describe the soulfully scorned individuals from a certain past closed-minded generation who struggle to deal with a new generation who are open minded, curious, informed and non-conforming when confronting the issues that might have brought them to where they are or are not in today's society.

Our forefathers and mothers were taught to have public moral decency and accommodating hearts no matter whose skull was being cracked in their sleep the night before. Despite the rapes, mindless beatings and verbal and social abuses sustained by powerless family members, they were taught to turn a deaf ear to logic in order to maintain the appearance of the ideal Christian family to people who are themselves struggling to function. Because our forefathers and mothers were never given an identity by their parents, they were forced to navigate (at least in the Black community) through the issues of life aimlessly in order to have a glimpse of an idea of who and what they should be. They had to go out and seek permission from others to be recognized as mere human beings, grown adults and simply relevant before they went home to their children. They didn't always make it.

I speak as an offspring of that generation. We no longer have the luxury of closing our eyes. So being forced to see what I would have preferred to ignore, I am compelled to admit my faults, weaknesses as well as theirs because my eyes have been forced wide open, I now have these painful thorns I wish I didn't have. These insane wounds that passed down to me, without the anticipation of my transformation, could only serve to cripple me and teach me the looming pessimism that comes with slavery.

Life would be so much easier if I would not have to deal with them, but then, again, my child would. This is my letter to them. Thank you for enduring.

20
"Thorns"
07.09.02

I love you
But I've taken offense.
No, you cannot go through another day blameless,
It doesn't make any sense.
I'm looking through the rose bushes
For what has become 'my discarded heart'.
I'm looking past your well wishes
Past the pretty part.
A winter window exposes the coldness
That ignites the apathy in your inner being.
Your denial has been my coffin.
You never wanted to spend any time with me really seeing
What has thwarted me often.
Did you bring me here just to leave me?
What could have had you captivated?
I often wondered…could you see me?
I'm sorry, but I get so aggravated!
This pain in my gut is twisting and churning
I'm looking to you for salvation
Your compassion is missing,
My God, I'm hurting!
Where were you when I needed you?
Remember when I pleaded with?
Are you here now or are you too busy?
That's ok. I'll wait. I know you love me,
Just know it's making me dizzy.
I need you and no, it isn't silly,
Nor is it funny.
This isn't about your status
Nor is it even about the money.

It doesn't matter anymore
What you say you intended
I'm feeling your childhood pain.
Please listen, your child is offended.
You said you never had pain
And I swear I don't know why.
Am I just a thorn of this red rose
Plucked from your side?
I never grew from rain, my existence denied.
Simply left to bleed and bleed again
And to be left here in need again…
So here I am, your child, indeed.
Indeed again.

Introduction 21

"We Are Our Own Daddy"

When do we gain real power, and at what age? When others point a finger at us, feeling as though they've exposed us, are we supposed to change? Or does real power or change occur when we've begun to point the finger at ourselves? And what would be the purpose at pointing the finger at ourselves? Is there a purpose at pointing the finger at each other?

These are the questions I would like for the members of the finger pointing age to ask themselves. I want you to ask yourselves as you reflect on your own adolescence. Know that the only way to help young people is to use empathy instead of judgment. I also want the younger generation to answer the questions presented above. Know that your disconnection from authority and leadership, without excuse, will lead to your demise.

If you stay focused on sagging pants, tattoos and music you will miss the real generation you've helped to create. We have a generation of young people who either will lead or follow. They want to follow people who genuinely are invested in leading them to a promised land. This isn't something new; you also wanted the same thing. You just didn't have to search as hard to find it. Take a moment and explore with me a mindset of adolescent maturity that will push you beyond the finger pointing and calling out of what has already been declared a generation of juvenile delinquents. Listen as the voices of our youth ask you to quit pushing and begin to lead them into our future.

21
"We Are Our Own Daddy"

Our generation is the generation you kept telling us we'd be
But, you didn't lead us into the proud
You didn't lead us into the brave or even into the free
No, we got here on our own strength
After you became distracted
You told us to fly like eagles, only with our claws retracted
So now, we don't have any real nest
Or anything we've clung to
Now we don't hear our own mothers
And we have no fathers to run to
We're unconventional, we're uncompromising
And we hate to ever lose
We have more options, choices
And more pathways to choose
You sang all day long how you believed
We children were your future
Yet, you taught us to get it for ourselves
Without even so much as a tutor
Maybe we weren't the future yet, you hadn't shown us how
You let the TV raise us and the media are our parents now.
Our claws are retracted, nowhere to grab hope
We've always felt fractioned,
And sold off like homemade soap
But, we can't totally blame your generation
No, some of the blame we must take for ourselves
Because we've ignored every conversation
We only sought what we've known as wealth.
We've chosen to disconnect
And become what we've somehow deemed as special
We've chosen to reject your wisdom
And opted for only hard-knock lessons

Today, we have no real foundations
A place in which we respect, or for that matter, derive
All we're left with is this self-serving ignorance in our lives
And as much as we hate to admit it, you were right.
The music we've listened to has actually become our God…
And our light.
It is the barometer in which we've placed
All of your words against.
We let it become the gate,
And now it becomes the whole fence.
We became our own daddy. We couldn't listen to anyone
And still we're very saddened
That we couldn't listen to anyone.
"Tell me, what would have been a father's purpose?
And what would having a real father have brought us?
What would have been the benefit
Beyond his financial service?"
I'm just speaking of what you taught us.
To me, a father is just a paycheck delivered by a free spirit
His title brings me no images of respect –
I feel no reverence when I hear it.
How can I begin to trust a God who says He is the Father?
Why would I think He'd be there for me?
I can't allow myself to accept the offer.
I have had my own fathering
All answers have come from me
While this thought of a Heavenly Father
Has continued to bother me
I want so much to be free
"Can I trust Him?
Can I release my own ways of parenting?
Will He never leave us?
Doe He really know how to care for me?
Does He really need us?
Or are we just a part of a charity?"
Being our own daddy totally separates us from the Father
We're unprotected and uncovered
Like dumb cattle driven to the slaughter
Yet, we know we need more than just a mother
We need a father. We need a cover.

Introduction 22

"Out Of Love"

I've often thought of all the things I would want to say to my ex-wife without all the bitterness and hurt we could easily afflict upon each other. What would I want her to know about how I feel now, in a real adult moment when we aren't holding each other hostage to the past? What would start her on the road to real recovery and healing just for herself so that she could move on and have a productive love life in the future? I find myself not wanting to pretend any longer that she didn't affect me in every way. She was a part of my life and my growth and I can't change any of that. If our goal in life is to give, to empower people to be better, to foster permission to overcome one's past, then it is up to us to begin with those in our past.

By inference, *Out of Love* has several connotations. On one hand, it signifies that I am no longer *in* love – tied to that which forces me to compromise or make concessions for the sake of the one to whom my heart is tethered. I have no contractual duty to fulfill or any legal obligation that requires me to consult with or get approval from a partner in whose life, in which, I no longer exist. It means the thing that drove me well beyond my limits in desert heat without so much as a sip of water to wet my ego, is no longer behind the wheel.

The penetrating pressure of that truth mandates that everything I portray and every word I relay from this point forward be done *Out of Love*. My life is a force to be reckoned with because the freedom that accompanies truth is replete with power. I now possess the ability to relate from a place of purity and of peace.

22
"Out Of Love"
05.09.97

We fell off the top of the cake
And now we're paying for our mistakes
Years of happiness down the drain
A broken marriage, full of pain
Too late for a cure or a compromise
Falling out of love and it's no surprise
Going our separate ways to start again
Hopefully trying to part as friends
Breaking old habits, leaving our comfort zone
Wondering if we can make it all alone
Praying for strength that the hurt will soon pass

Needing a shoulder to cry on
But not sure who to ask
By trusting in God and doing His will
Before we know it our hearts will soon heal
Starting a new life without one another
Trying to get through life
Each of us fully recovered
I really miss you and all of the good days
I'll never stop wishing things went a different way

It's over and done.
No use crying over spilt milk
Regrets, let's have none.
We have new lives to fulfill
Take care of yourself and watch what you do
Remember, I'm always a part of you.

Introduction 23

"A Sober Revelation"

Inspired by the thought of a young man learning to know and love himself for the first time. I once had a conversation with a young man who was in a treatment facility in which I worked in Kansas City, Missouri. I could hear in his voice the desperation for anyone who would have a different prospective on life and offer him an alternative. After he told me his story, he received my responsive lecture as a good son would from his father.

It's my opinion that young men aren't eager to destroy our communities with stupidity; they just don't have men who will take the time to really father them and not end up bragging about their own destruction of women and communities with their numerous sexual conquests in a deceptive effort to help them.

In the setting of this poem he is probably on the phone with her the day after they've had a sexual encounter with each other that left him satisfied as usual. However, when he finds himself at an odd and precarious position at home – alone, washing off the remnants of the night before and the scent of the girl who really feels like he loves her; an even bigger problem appears in his own mirror. He cannot look at himself.

He wakes up to a new day full of the promises of life, but is now challenged with the feelings and emotions he ignored just a few hours before. In the moment, he feels compelled to explore a different side of himself. And, for the first time, looks at her as a beloved sister – a woman with a heart; instead of a physical distraction to his inadequate understanding of himself and who he really is.

These feelings have begun to reaffirm the reality of neglect he experienced in his childhood. His current memory is triggered by the many times she tried to offer him her heart and true essence. His manipulative response to her has always been one that ended in his own gratification. In the end, he realizes this time he can't run. He is inspired to become a different man; and risks losing his 'easy sex partner to gain an ounce of integrity so that he can finally experience a level of self-respect he was never taught. As a result, he is empowered to become the man he always wanted to be… just by looking in the mirror and having a sober revelation.

23
"A Sober Revelation"
02.11.01

What we called a relationship based on trust,
Turned out to be a relationship based on lust.
And, girl, now I must confess
That all we had was sex!
The first thing that we did
Was to practice having kids.
Seems we had nowhere to go,
Tried to have a house without a home.
I didn't even ask you for your love;
And it should have been a must.
What you gave me was enough
I didn't even ask you for your trust.
It was easy to believe
That for companionship you were desperate.
My wants and your needs
I never really had to keep separate.
You settled for what easily became a cheap thrill
And so did I.
Nothing about our so-called love was real
It was potentially a high-priced lie.
So anyway,
I'm trying not to sound pathetic
But, when you asked me to stay with you
It sounded kind of poetic,
I didn't know why. I already had my way with you.
Remember, you did everything you could just to get with me.
Even if you had to sacrifice your virginity.
You couldn't even show it when you were upset with me
As long as it led to sex with me.
But, don't get me wrong; it's not all your fault.

When you said you were vulnerable and in pain,
I saw you as gullible and an easy gain.
Although, today is the day I don't like; it's the morning after.
And usually hiding from myself is what I choose to practice.
And I've had to look in the mirror
The real man inside of me
Made me see this whole thing a little clearer.
In this mirror I've looked mostly against my own will.
You can't imagine how inside, I really feel.
Every time I look at my handsome face
I see yours and it brings handsome disgrace.
You see, I'm sobered up from my lustful intoxication.
So, for once I'll be a man and make this proclamation.
I'm sorry.
I now realize that I could have protected your honor
And been your friend.
You could have talked to me from day's break to day's end.
Your body was not celebrated with Godly conviction;
I saw it as a threat to me and some sort of contradiction!
I was trying my best to conquer your body.
The more we did it, you were no longer Godly!
So, I'm asking you to forgive me and accept my apology.
I want so much, to be disciplined; I don't want to be slave
Not just within my body, but all of me
The man in me wants to behave.
Talking about love, I now understand
If anyone loves you that means they love…you.
And there will be no unreasonable demands
It doesn't mean you owe them anything
Or that you even have to be with them.
Sometimes it leads to an exchange of rings
Or just a cup of coffee with cream with them.
I've learned that I can love you from across the room
And if I cross the room maybe that is an act against love.
For anything that is predestined to honestly bloom
You will always be tested for what it's made of.
We are a people that still believe
That if you love me you've got to stay with me
Or I'll never let you go
Or even, you belong to me.
You may have heard it in a song
Or saw it in a show.

I declare now, I want what's best for you
And now, what's best for me.
It's my job to invest in you
While you invest in me.
Today, I explore every possibility
Of building a healthy relationship with myself.
I am open to the possibility
Of both of our hearts being kept.
So, now I'm confident that I've turned over a new leaf
It gives me great consolation and relief
That just knowing that the thing that releases me from my shame and degradation
Is knowing I've had… a sober revelation.

Introduction 24

"A Bastard's Breakfast"

Most see this word, 'bastard' as a purely intended insult and a judgment of their family dynamics. I certainly do understand that. The word 'bastard' here denotes a willful type of rejection of fatherhood and mentorship. Many women today have rejected the romantic relationships because they have been hurt by them in the past. Many of those relationships have resulted in women having children by the very men who caused their heartbreak. In an effort to save themselves after a gut-wrenching separation filled with anger, some mothers have presented fathers as negative, powerless and pathetic men to their children. In turn, those children grew up dispelling the worth and necessity of natural fathers (or even surrogate coverings) in their lives. The result is a life of all answers coming from them and their relative generation. This is not acceptable.

As long as God is Father, we are not free to exit out of the family structure, regardless of our dismay, and into our own abyss, justifying our own pain and misunderstandings. We must allow ourselves to be as good little children and be molded by those commissioned by God to speak into our lives and direct us in the name of the Father. A life lived based upon the excuses built from a false right not to have a father is a Godless existence. Every young person, every mother, every older person who grew up without a father, I believe, will not be excused as a victim, but held accountable for not finding a surrogate father-figure to at least, periodically speak into their lives.

As a child, and an only son I needed to be able to identify with my father. Now, I must say that I am fortunate to be one of those people who grew up with his father, and a wonderful father at that. My parents never divorced. I'm very grateful for that. But, my father grew up in the time when men didn't talk to their kids, they provided for them. Every weekend my father would go about doing the tasks that good fathers do and I was left at home with my mother. My mother would always encourage him to take me with him. But, my father didn't have a clue how to talk to me, even though he loved me. He proceeded to try to find other ways to have a 'relationship' with me.

Now, don't ask me how I knew to do this, but I'm relaying it to you as advice; I decided that I wanted to be with my father. I didn't want anything from him, not wanting him to buy me anything or even spend money on me; I just wanted to go with him. I loved being around him, even if he didn't know how to talk to me. Sooo…I got in the car and began talking to him…..NON-STOP!! This made my dad very uncomfortable, but he starting coming around; laughing at my silliness, my constant questions and eagerness to be with him. It's like my father was fathered by his son. Today, my father and I have the closest relationship I could have ever dreamed of. I'm a son who did not make excuses, but went after my dad and found my father.

24
"A Bastard's Breakfast"
01.03.12

A man sits with his mentor day after day
He sits with his friend eating breakfast outside, it's May
Not concerned about the birds
Or the other sounds in the air
He's not hearing my words
He's not giving much of a care.
It's summer now and the season is well at hand
It's still not about what I can tell him that I know
It's coming down to only what he thinks he can stand.
He's listening to his own ideas and preplanned destruction
I know every time we're together,
I seem to have tickets to his production.
We've run ashore and it's run its course
Our breakfast has become only about what he will endorse.
We share glimpses, droplets and worthless moments
He can't accept simple compromises and wise components
We tether back and forth, making a dawned construction
And we struggle needlessly, having limited discussions.
I nearly beg him to listen just like a good son could
While ideas pop off in his head like a loaded gun would
His mind is parented by a bastard's new notions
A sign to me that disaster is his new focus.
Maybe I can't help him, while he helps himself
To the music video life
To the easiest wealth
Why waste time with a man who is settled in independence?
One who has nothing beyond his commitment to your dependence?
If I can't help mend you, I should not try to help send you
If you can't find my logic and impression
There is no way that I could defend you

You will never understand our intended connection.
You will misuse all my guidance and affection
I am not your father by biological standards
So I'm not bothered by illogical banter
If you want your bastard status
And all that your uncoverings brings with it
I will allow you your freedom
Because I release your privilege
And I say to you...
If you're going to block your blessings...
Finish your breakfast.

Introduction 25

"All Day It Rained"

Often we want to only bask in the warmth of sunshine until the glorious setting of the sun. It's true, there's nothing more comforting than a beautiful breezy sun-filled day you get to enjoy. Most shun the prospect of a rainy day and all that it brings. We see rain in the natural as a reason to stay home – hazardous, troublesome and just down-right unwelcome. In nature, it is an absolute necessity. What makes the sunshine so wonderful? The rainy days we've endured. What makes trees and flowers so strong and colorful? The rain. What makes us all grow and change and really happy? Don't you know? It's the rain.

In my life I've endured lots of rain. There were days when I was embarrassed because I knew people didn't understand why I never seemed to come out from under the cloud of rain in my life. It's funny how when people meet you when you're down; they tend to think that's who you are. Some of us get periodic rain. Some get sprinkles or even downpours at times. This rain was consistent, retarding any movement. But its aim was nothing but sheer purpose. It was designed to bring destiny, but only when it was finished.

25
"All Day It Rained"
2009

All day it rained ...
As though collective clouds were pleased to empty out
All the pain left by the sorrows of the passing season
All day it rained...
As though halted emotions escaped with tears and mourning
Of an entire nation whose children had been slain
All day it rained...
And I felt the stirring of blood stained grass and the weight of the stone marked by man's senseless acts of fear toward each other
All day it rained...
As I watched remnants of memories steadily wash away seasons of times good and bad, of failures and successes
All day it rained...
Telling of the capacity of God's grace and compassion and His roaring anger
All day it rained...
In my life drowning purpose and destiny
Through showers of conflict and contradiction
All day it rained...
Turning my weeks into months and months into years
All day it rained...
Until my will had given over to the will of the passing season
All day it rained...
And I felt my soul prepare for a clear transformation
All day it rained...
Until the ground was moist and fertile with heaven's seed!
All day it rained...
Until the air was filled with soil and a blooming, living essence!
All day it rained...
Until I saw the breaking through of tiny rosebuds and blades of grass!

All day it rained...
Until life began to grab hold of the soil with a strangling grip!
All day it rained...
Until one by one my trees began to grow strong with branches stretched to the heavens!
All day it rained...
Until I could sprout out leaves and moisture, it's how I breathed!
All day it rained...
While my roots dug deep and my trunk became fuller and denser!
All day it rained...
Until I was tall and relevant and could command substance!
All day it rained...
Until I could tell of the fierce storms that were coming just by swaying!
All day it rained...
Until the sky was filled with bright colors leading from one place to a better place!
All day it rained....
And it poured ...
And it rained,
And it poured,
And it rained,
And it poured,
Until I was...here.

Introduction 26

"Blue Ocean Sky"

You may not have noticed; then again, perhaps you have, days when the sky is in its bluest form. No clouds, no streaks, no other colors, just blue. Not just blue, but the bluest blue you've ever seen. Suddenly, you're overcome with that feeling that maybe…just maybe… everything's going to be all right. You may not open your mouth to say a word; you may not even pause, but you notice it. In that moment, you cannot imagine anything bad coming your way. In fact, you cannot remember any of the bad you have already encountered. I want you to fearlessly see the love you're in like this, at least for a moment. Fully embrace your bluest days; you may need them to win against your cloudiest. The power of the present and being in the now is greater than what was or could be because it's now; and right now is everything and everything is all right.

It's blue, like an uncharted **clear** body of Caribbean water. The warmth is encased in the richness of its color and fluidity. And like the ocean, whether day or night, it is complimented by the gentleness of warm winds. Similar to the love you may crave, I had a moment about the love that I imagine…

26
"Blue Ocean Sky"

And as far as the eye can see
As far as I am concerned
I believed in the love of you and me
And everything we've learned.
I treasure these molten moments
That brings life to the ocean laid
In these moments we've laid together,
In these moments that we've together owned
In the hours that will soon make days,
To the sands' morning glaze.
The ocean's foam
Lines the blue ocean's sky
Its bluest hues
Designs that opens lives.
We walk along the paths that mark our divinity
Disconnected from what may hold us to our humanity
That connection that lies in the mouths of our grandmothers
A blue ocean sky is set as the backdrop,
All too often, the black plot
To all of those movie lies.
The blue of the sky
Is the opposite of an indigo night
Blue in pallet
Blue in reason
My ocean is calloused
Because you're still the meanest.
When you're angry and won't speak to me
Disconnected….
And then disconnect again
Until all the colors match
And you've labeled wind…

Make the blue sky spin.
Blue Ocean Sky again
My Blue Ocean night sigh, Baby
Our Blue Ocean then.

Introduction 27

"Buried Alive"

Do not fool yourself into believing there aren't people who hate you simply because you exist. They honestly wish that you will stop breathing. They seem to grab a shovel full of dirt every time you're near. There may be many reasons why these people hate you. The most significant of those reasons is that they truly don't believe God is who He says He is. They are somehow convinced that God is not vast enough to have room for every single person to have value. Or that God is powerful enough to distribute gifts to every man. Consequently, they continue to fight for positions, money and favor; all of the things that God freely provides.

These people are extremely angry because it appears that you have too many gifts, too much favor, too much promise or even too much potential. They believe it is unfair that the two of you do not share similar plights in life and they believe that they are experiencing more adversity than triumphs. Their eyes are so fixed on you that they cannot see God, let alone be grateful for any day-to-day victories.

Imagine if you will, a teacher passing out milk and cookies to a group of grade schoolers. Each child is grateful and excited for their two cookies and carton of milk; that is, until they see some of their classmates with three cookies. They immediately feel short-changed; believing that one more cookie means a better experience and a greater reward. At the same time and without any other variables, they immediately feel it is unfair that anyone receives more than they do. But instead of asking the teacher for another cookie, they become so fixated on the belief that their classmates should NOT have more cookies than they do. You watch as their short-lived enthusiasm is quickly swallowed up by

envy. A temper tantrum ensues! Little do they know that once you go after the one thing that someone else has, you run the risk of losing every thing that
you have. And within minutes, the teacher took both their cookies and milk.

Substance without gratitude is nothing. We live with far too many adults who have never learned this fundamental principle. As such, their lives are just as predictably devious, envious and covetous as the above-mentioned elementary students. Know that your favor with people is a problem for the envious, the haters, and the jealous blockers that loom around you on a regular basis! Just look around; there are people who would rather see you be buried alive than to have what they feel is unfairly given to you.

27
"Buried Alive"
02.04.10
9:40a

It's not that you thought I was dead
It's more that you thought I was irrelevant.
Your speaking to me, to you,
Was more than kind.
It was down right benevolent.
I see now that you were intimidated
By what you perceived
Wouldn't just become one of your hired servants.
Or wouldn't bow down on my knees
It didn't faze me or even make me nervous!
Your sabotage and manipulations
Wasn't necessary, you just needed more patience.
People thought you were about numbers
No, you were really about fractions
You tried to rid yourself what
You thought was slow and unwise
You shoveled dirt, backhanded,
Right into my eyes.
And I soon became buried in an unmarked grave
Simply because I wouldn't be your slave.
Buried alive, I could still hear the sneers and the laughter
Systematically denied, while the scent of death was coming faster
I now understand that your attempts of terror
Ultimately cause you one fatal error.
Every thing you wanted death to bring me
Caused you to die a little everyday you were scheming
You were the one suffocating your own dreams.
Your dreams had nothing to do with this shoveling theme
Did you ever wonder why every stick and stone you threw,

Went under the coffin and the ground beneath me grew!?
Did you ever wonder why
After spreading hatred and spreading lies,
In my grave I didn't die?
Did you ever wonder what kept me alive?
While in this grave, my breath was not denied?
In this grave, I was still connected to the Vine.
This Vine extended beyond my grave
Right through the coffin in which I was laid.
It was rich with nutrients and vitamins
My Father knew He would be invited in.
It was charged with God's presence and oxygen!
The power that is no match for this box I'm in.
Jesus is that Vine!
He is not subject to the elements
He is not subject to time!
He won't let you hold me to my crime!
He has a problem with me being buried alive
When I call Him, He will arrive.
He is my Father and He won't let you hold me.....
He is my friend. He won't hold me to the old me.
Buried alive. And alive being the optimum word.
Your pre-occupation with it is not productive
To God, it's nothing short of absurd.
Stop watching my cookies and go get your own!
For some reason you believe your blessing is a loan
As long as you keep trying to bury me
You will have to keep on worrying
That you will run out of time
To keep me from being alive.

Introduction 28

"Don't Ask the Children"

Inspired by a conversation with a Residential Treatment Center client in Kansas City, Missouri who spoke to me about things his mother thought he didn't know or wouldn't talk to him about. This young man began to confide in me how his mom had been with many men. He went on to say that it was not unusual to wake up to half-dressed men – strangers in his home. Without question, he would acquiesce and try to mind or respect these men because that's what 'Mama' had instructed. These different men tried to try to father him in exchange for sex with his mother. He watched as these men repeatedly used his mother in a variety of ways; and broke her heart until she was morally bankrupt and emotionally shattered.

He continued to talk in a matter-of-fact-like tone. Apparently, at some point his mother arbitrarily decided to write off men. She now has a live in girlfriend the kids were told to call "Aunt Susie". The children of the household are not only supposed to accept this drastic change, but they are also expected to understand their mother's radical decision. Like most children, and without exception, this young man wanted to please his mom. So he spent all of his efforts and energies in doing just that.

During the conversation I asked him how he really felt about it all. At first, he was adamant about his defense of her actions. But when I asked him how he was handling it, how it made him feel and his opinion, he paused for a moment; and without warning began to cry uncontrollably. As I comforted him, it seems that no one had ever taken a personal interest in what affect it all had on him. This time, speaking honestly and through years of pain, he told me how he hated his mother for always making other men a priority and relegating him to the position of second place. And then to require the unspeakable in gender preference after all he had accepted was almost more than he could bear.

Wasn't it enough that he had no choice but to grow up living with demonically-influenced sex-starved strangers exercising authority and control over his every move? All the while, all his mother was looking for was love. Its impact was severe in his life. His mother, along with every other person who was allowed to rule clearly forgot that with each passing day this young man as well as his other siblings were becoming products of the environment they were forced to endure. So this poem is a voice for children who love their mothers, but who dare not hurt them by saying what they really feel.

He was better that day for being able to finally be heard…

28
"Don't Ask the Children"

Oh, really? Is that what you've decided to do?
Well, I guess you are grown
And it's really your choice to choose;
Especially when that's what the world condones,
You don't want to lose.
But, if you will; give me a moment
To explain something from a new prospective
Oh, yes, I'm going to get into it
So, I want you to beware, your pride may not be protected.
Maybe no one has made it apparent
Could be no one has made it clear
That your child has made you a parent
Even if it started with a simple beer.
Oh, yeah. It's all right.
It might have been fun.
You spent the whole time creating an atmosphere
At least, until the sex was done.
Validating your worth through the moans of sexual conquests.
Because the moment is where you chose to invest.
I guess your child was born with those issues they now display
Yet you ignore the fact that they miss you, miss you every day.
Baby, Mama's got to get her party on, too!!
Are the abusive words that came from you.
But what have you really created?
Oh, my God! What have you really done?
Nine months later and he or she ain't fine no more
And two months into it you're asking folks what child support is for.
You don't hear your children.
You don't want to know how they feel.
Don't ask the children.
Because what they tell you will be real.

No, I don't mean the babies and kiddies
And the little ones playing on the floor.
They would be too easy,
Too easy to ignore.
No. Ask the ones you keep calling 'stupid' and 'dumb'
Ask the ones you call 'gangbangers', go ahead, ask your son.
Talk to the one you keep 'giving up to Jesus'
And giving over to a reprobated mind.
Realize that from home, he wouldn't be leaving
If at home, <u>you'd</u> keep <u>your</u> behind!
And if that girl appears to be a 'hellion'
Remember when you raised her
You raised her in own your rebellion.
What do your children think of your lifestyle?
Can they talk about you at school with a smile?
What do they know about your bedroom?
Do they know where your condoms are?
Or is the fact that Aunt Susie's sleeping with mommy
To anybody else, considered bizarre?
What's mommy gonna do when the child support checks don't come?
When she charges her new outfit
Will she get mad at us again
When daddy makes her feel dumb?
Why do I have so many stepbrothers and sisters?
And why don't all of them live with me?
I know I'm not supposed to ask these questions
But, these are the things I see.
How do I be a man, mommy?
Why do you hate dad so much?
Should I hate him too, mommy?
Because I love him so much.
Do you love my stepbrother more than me
Because you love his dad?
My stepbrother loves me, mommy
He's all I ever had.
And one last question, please, mommy.
Why are you always so mad?
I know,... we'll pray to Jesus on our knees, mommy
That He will make both of us glad!

Introduction 29

"Improbable"

Not afraid anymore of things that seem unreachable. I'm not dealing with natural things the way I used to. So, my life has come to this.... The things that have evaded me are occurring. If I had listened to people who only live in the natural, I would have been subject to what they thought of my capabilities. Everything about me has exceeded the expectations of most. Oh well...their loss. I'm being myself, the man I was born to be.......extraordinary.

However, this probability didn't come as a surprise to me. I've understood my destiny since I was a child. Undoubtedly, there are countless children who have also tapped in their life's purpose. What is unfortunate are the adults present in their lives who, because of their own regret, fear the impenetrable greatness that exists in their children.

Who then is the improbable? Is it me or you? Truthfully, it should be neither. It is high time we stop sentencing anyone; and rally together to make the improbable, probable. No fear, just love. Children that are considered problem children and appear to have 'no direction' are usually those children who God has touched with 'a little something extra'. Don't discount them; guide them. Let go, let God take care of the rest. Be the songs you sing about. Be the sermons you 'amen' to. Become the church in your own heart, and not the building. Become the love you need and not merely a vessel of love to others. Break molds! Challenge clichés! Break curses! Walk away from stereotypes. Let go. Let go. Let go.

29
"Improbable"

Been busy daily dying
Been dizzily daily trying
To find and figure out
What is the song of me,
What's wrong with me
And why I am living without.
I've felt imprisoned by the improbability
So, I'm giving lately blindly
And I'm freely dating timing
I'm following my assignment
Now, it's no longer private
I've got a testimony
And nothing about it is phony
And it's that God didn't leave me lonely
He was there with me only.
Through all the tests and pain
Through massive mud slides and unimaginable fits of rain
I've got an improbable dreaming awakening
To an unsolvable thing I've been facing.
I confess, my victory is nigh me
I confess, my lips will be finding
Words that empower and give me life
Words that devour the enemy's ties.
Words that deliver my money forever!
Words that give me colorful feathers!
The word is nigh me and gives me life
The worst is behind me as I turn to Christ
It's possible that I will love
It's possible that I will succeed
It's possible that I will run
Toward all that love brings.

I am the probable
Awaken from the improbable
I am unstoppable!
As I spread my best wings.

Introduction 30

"JESUS DID A BACK FLIP"

Make no mistake about it, I'm writing in support of the preservation of the manner of worship that brought all of us to the place where we can now worship in a more true understanding of who Christ is. I am appalled at some of the tactics and self-serving tantrums some call worship in today's society.

Who is this new 'minister' and who does he work for? Jesus? I don't think so. Someone hired this person who has absolutely no respect for the Lord beyond what is acceptable to his audience of innocent ill-informed parishioners.

I guess Jesus' dying on a cross was a mere thang He did uh, fo yo' love and yo' entertainment. How can one compare this new-aged system of theatrics to the solemn allegiance from our forefathers and mothers that brought us over!? Trust me; I know that I would be eagerly dismissed by those who are the perpetrators of this sort of thing in the name of today's young people. But, young people aren't new to the planet! There have been young people around since Adam and Eve had children! So did they love God then…and if so, why? Did they turn to God then, and if so, then why? What if they didn't immediately turn to-God? I have never seen anyone successful at encouraging me to come toward better, acting like worse! I don't need you to be more like me in order to help me be more like Christ! Do the Christians go smoke with the smokers to encourage them, or lay down with prostitutes to lead them to Christ? Do you cut your wrists in order to keep the ones you love from committing suicide? The Bible says, "With love and kindness will I draw you." Love and kindness, is that so difficult?

It says nothing about loud, suspect, suggestive music, pizza parties and dance offs in order to pledge some allegiance to Jesus. When Jesus, himself made disciples, he told them to turn from everyone, expect to suffer for his name sake, then he led them to a death-burial-and-resurrection for His name sake! His commandment for us is to love thy neighbor! Is there some misunderstanding? Clearly, love and kindness is the vehicle through which people are drawn. Following the life He lived on earth, believing His word and in His second coming is the mission and directive given by our Lord. Neither the modality nor the validity of the meaning has changed. God meant exactly what He said. Why have we added potato chips and sodas, tight jeans, baseball caps and designer sneakers, gifts and free stuff to the mix as a means of coercion? Have we become con artists? I've witnessed meetings with perspective youth leaders who were instructed to *like what they like, befriend them by going to their schools and buy their lunches; like their music, buy them shoes, etc... Essentially, breaking down their resistance!*

After more than 20 years working with youth who have struggled within the juvenile justice system, this method of approach looks really familiar. This type of youth leadership is eerily similar to the profile of a person who manipulates children into submission; seducing children. In the youth care industry, it is known as "grooming". I say to the leaders and all youth departments, no more! Stop it! If you don't truly believe in Jesus (AS IS), stop perpetrating an image! Please, for the sake of our young, read your Bible and recommit yourself to Jesus before influencing someone to look up to and follow you. Check your history, and then rework your approach. Pull your pants back up and walk worthy of the vocation to which you have been called. Lead young people to Jesus, not your career. Jesus paid it all; and it is finished! Stop putting clown paint on Him and demanding back flips for entertainment!!!

30
"JESUS DID A BACK FLIP"

While the blood is streaming down His torn and ripped back,
While He is blinded by the blood and dirt pooling in His eyes,
While He is enduring the thorns deeply embedded into His skull,
While His organs are being pierced and severed and exposed,
While He hemorrhages and bleeds internally,
While He struggles to comprehend the pain in His feet and hands from the nails that have broken His bones,
While He struggles to keep consciousness so that He can still look at the ones He loved mock Him,
While He struggles to keep Himself upon that Cross and not die too soon,
While His muscles ache from being ripped apart from carrying a cross 8 times His size to the top of a hill,
While His skin and flesh peel and fall away from His body as a result from the beatings and whippings,
While spit and mucus from the mouths of people who hate Him runs down His torn body and orifices,
While He is mocked and cursed and was called a liar and a thief,
While He hangs there humiliated and exposed because of His nakedness,
While He hung there and died.
While His father watched in horror……
You asked Him to do a back flip:
"Our young people need you to dance a little, Jesus.
They need you to do a little rap. Wzup? Come on, Dude!
Can You wear some 'fly' shoes or turn Your hat to the back or something?
Can You show them a little 'bling' since You got it like that with Your Dad?
Maybe You can kick somebody's butt or cut someone's ear off or something.

Can You just do something cool? They ain't gon' love You if that Cross thang is all You got!!
I know! How about a back flip?!? Ninja stuff?? Work with me, Jesus. Young people would be sure to love You then.
Maybe then, they would even follow You.
Yes, You could get in line with some of the celebrities who have really done some awesome things!
Maybe then, Your life would have stood for something.
Come on, Jesus…. Can You do one back flip?"
"Hat to da' back! Jeans saggin' down!
Got dem' Jordans one time fo' yo' mind!
I'm holdin' da' mic with a rapper's grip, baby!
Ya' see me? Ya' see me?!?
What, what! Can I get a WWJD?"
Holla atcha boi! Uh oh, hold on!...
Jesus done did a back flip fo' yo' love!"
And then He hung His head…….and died.

Introduction 31

"My Great Father"

I've been called a minority most of my life because I was born African American. It is a label that I am supposed to exclusively accept because of someone's count of Black people in America. Needless to say, I'm offended by that and do not accept. But, I am a minority in another sense. I have a great father.

My dad, who isn't perfect, is a great man who I have ALWAYS seen as a king! It's not so much what he says, but his regal way of saying nothing and commanding so much in it!! When he speaks everyone gets silent – giving their undivided attention to a man capable of crowning his audiences with wisdom, and knighting them with favor. Even during what some would see as the winter season of his life, he has the heart of a 17 year old and the wisdom of a 117 year old. I'm right where I need to be because of his example. He is a great man to many people; and a greater man still to his children.

I learned to be a worshipper because of my father. Most people acquire this ability from their mothers. But I was blessed to have the head, the CEO, the pastor of our house lead with humility and honor. As a child, it was not unusual to see my father bowed at the altar of the church in worship, giving thanks to God. Other men, wrapped in the pride of their own ego, refused to assume a similar posture in the presence of such a mighty God.

I watched in awe as he laid the foundation for the man I would become. Perhaps Dad was thanking God for me. Maybe he was offering prayers on my behalf. Whatever the cause or case, I get it! And I'm grateful. My ears and eyes absorbed every detail. I even sat on the front row during church services to avoid distractions; and to soak up as much of the preached Word as possible. Clearly, I wanted to be just like my dad, who obviously loved Jesus.

I desperately wanted to know this Jesus who had captured his heart. I admit there was a time when I wanted to be just like my father (as any son should). Now, I no longer want that. I do want my father to see me as an extension of who he is and everything he wanted his son to become. I don't want to return to my father exactly what he gave me, but with more, with double, with the respect his sacrifice was due. I want him to know that his many sacrifices and consistency paid off. All the humiliation and pain he suffered, working for people who could never see his worth, was worth it. After all, he only has one son. I got you, Dad! Let our family name ring out and always be remembered as great! You are my great father!

31
"My Great Father"
06.03.10

My father is the strongest man I've ever known
And I am today, the strength he has sown.
I once was a child and now I'm full grown
There is no stronger man I've known.
My father walks in honor and humility
With assured authority such as in royalty.
A man with every reason to subdue life
And ravish the breath out of it for him self.
A man faithful and committed to his wife
A man whose family is his wealth.
Patient and kind, yet surprisingly unyielding and stern
Never overbearing and always willing to learn.
Masculine, yet youthful in making wise decisions
Careful, but truthful; my father won't compromise religion.
Sitting like a king on a throne made of Jasper and Jade
My father ruled his home with his heart and his thoughtful ways.
Intertwined and hopelessly in love with the woman who is his wife.
My dear mother, his morning, his noon, and his night.
Blessed is the man whose children have no doubt or question
What real love is and that giving is a lifelong lesson.
My Great Father, produced great children and with one grateful son.
My Great Father is consistent in that my soul shall overcome
Any tests that my lie before me and wait
For I am a true descendent of what is truly great.
A worshipper, disregarding what other men might do.
A follower of the word of Christ, so that he might add to you.
I learned that from you, Dad, and for righteousness I truly thirst
And that men, no matter what, should always praise first.
You are an example of how to rule your domain and your destiny
I will always long to present to him the good and only the best of me.

My father is a man of legacy,
A man who was bred in contradiction, coldness and severe poverty.
My father is a man of <u>regency</u>,
Who raised his children in confidence, warmth and in <u>sovereignty</u>.
I'm grateful, not just in part, but all of me.
You must know how I feel and have always felt.
To be his son is to possess the greatest wealth.
My Great Father....
I'm so very proud of you.
I honor you, Dad, and I love you.

Introduction 32

"My Parent's Porch"

This is the true story of the beauty of the porch of my childhood. Going back to visit my parents, I am comforted even more by sharing mornings and afternoons with them, reminiscing about the past and telling them about our plans for the future. Watching them beam with pride. We often talked about fishing and their grandchildren and the church we grew up in. Then, as always, my parents' turn to each other with dreamy eyes and express their love. That porch may not have been perfect, but it was perfect for us. There have been countless visitors on that porch, sitting and sharing their lives – laughing with us, crying with us, learning with us on sunny days, on cloudy days and sometimes at night. Come with me as I share with you this staple of my childhood, My Parent's Porch.

32
"My Parents' Porch"

Three beautiful arches and one breezeway
Help frame the most glorious mornings you've ever experienced
For a Saturday morning that more than easily attracts the world
My dad sits as the king of fishermen pondering his latest catch
My mom joins him, just to be with him.
Hours pass by as neighbors walk by and wave a familiar Hello.
My parent's porch, a place shielded by prayer from the changing world around them.
I remember the fire hydrant in the distant edge of the yard
Stands as a guard, through the left arch.
I remember we had a 25 mph speed limit sign posted in our yard,
partially covered up by the hanging limbs of the mighty tree
whose roots dug up our sidewalk.
My mom had plants hanging from the archways.
I remember standing on the black rod iron railings in those archways as a kid.
The wrap around porch was surrounded by thick green grass that was my father's pride and joy.
Friends and loved ones would come by to visit and hoped they could sit on that porch.
It is a place of contemplation, resolution, query and wisdom.
The wisdom usually came from the fisher king.
The love came from his wife.
My sisters go there to sit at my parent's feet and gain wisdom, direction and support.
Everything you've been looking for can be found on my parent's porch.
With a hot cup of coffee or a warm cup of tea
On the other end of the porch, you can watch the sunset as cars begin to slow down, the evening gets quieter.
My parent's porch has an incredible skyline where the sunrise and sunset are only matched by those of tropical resort hotels.

As time moves on, grandchildren came, and then great-grandchildren came
Pictures loom around the house of moments – events recorded on that porch
Many chairs, suitcases, briefcases, plants and even bird's nests
Have all made that archives of my parents' porch
Fish have been fried and even breakfast eaten on my parents' porch
We've seen the good, the bad and the ugly from that porch
Drawing us back into the kitchen for contemplation
I love this place.
It's one of a kind with one of a kind memories.

Introduction 33

"I Have To Dance Hard"

Yes, I am that guy who dances real hard when I used to go clubbing. I didn't know any better, I was just trying to get my groove on. Yes, I'm the church boy who is used to shouting and dancing like my shoes were on fire! When I got older, I went out to clubs and tried to dance the way I had secretly done at home many times before. To me, there is no substitute for dancing! I love it to this day. I just don't like clubs anymore. I would never drink, didn't need to. I believe the world would have far less stressed if they would just dance! I would feel the beat all the way down in my bones! I had no choice! I wouldn't even look at the other guys to see if I had their 'cool' approval. They must have hated me. In fact, I never understood why anyone would go to a place where the purpose and focus is dancing and then proceed to pretend to hate dancing! If I didn't come with a partner, I would ask random women to dance and to this day, I was NEVER turned down! So, this is a little of how I felt on some of the nights when I would go out.

33
"I Have To Dance Hard"

I have to dance hard!
Girl, I don't know how to groove
I like to dance hard, baby
I ain't got nothing to prove!
See ol' dude over there
Barely moving his feet?
I will dance circles around him
Baby, I own this beat!
Un-huh! This is my song!
Girl, every song is my jam!
I am the inventor of hard dance!
Girl, don't you know who I am?
When I first starting coming here
I used to really sweat
Now I can dance for hours
And never even get wet!
See, most girls can't hang with me.
I be making them sit down!
But, if you wanna do my thang with me
Baby, just stick around!
I have to dance hard!
And I celebrate the rhythm
My body's like a snake, girl
I slide and I slither!
You should try dancing hard
And put down that drink!
Leave a puddle of sweat
right where you are
When you leave here,
Baby, you should stink!
I dance hard! And I'd like to thank the DJ's

For breaking off some more power!
I dance hard! And I feel no pain
Until that last and final hour!
I dance harder when I dance!
I look retarded when I dance!
You look smarter when I dance!
I'm a secret farter when I dance!
I look slick when I dance!
I get chicks when I dance!
You'll be sick when I dance!
I might spit when I dance!
Baby, I do tricks when I dance!
Might turn flips when I dance!
We gon' dip when I dance!
Don't need no sip when I dance!
It ain't no joke when I dance!
You might choke when I dance!
You might have a stroke when I dance!
Getting soaked when I dance!
I dance hard, baby, I dance hard!

Introduction 84

"NEOPOLITAN"

I had the good fortune of being born between two sisters. Nice, huh? Who am I kidding? It was the breeding ground for mass quantities of estrogen-related whippings! I don't understand why I had to pick on them repeatedly, but I did. Some days I spent my time cherishing them and protecting them, other days I was Satan, the teaser, the bed wetter!

My oldest sister would chase me through the house threatening to kill me! I think a lot of our arguments and disagreements had something to do with the fact that I probably try to torment her boyfriends more than her. Oh, what fun that was! My younger sister was just too pale for me. I needed to see her turn red and scream at least three times a week! She seemed to hate everything I did, and it only pleased me to do what she hated more and more!

All this was probably because I didn't know how to handle the fact that I saw both of them as the most beautiful females I had ever seen. I couldn't understand why they were my sisters, at the same time I wanted to protect them with my life. So, I had the job of two or three brothers. What's a middle child to do? This is one brother's account of what it was like to be raised in the middle of one red-bone sister and one high yellow sister! This is dedicated to my beloved sisters, Michelle and Nicole.

34
"NEOPOLITAN"
02.02.10
11:11a

Oh, to be the chocolate
Between the apocalypse!
Behind the jabs and quips
To: "Don't kiss him with your greasy lips!"
Between strawberry and vanilla
Who would do that to a fella?
It's a recipe for mass quantities of drama!
The E.R. at a hospital
Couldn't compare to this trauma!
One sister older,
One sister younger.
Both very beautiful,
I always had to be their thunder.
Their boyfriends always looked at me crazy
They said, "Looka here, baby…
Can you get your skinny brother?
You already have a father and a mother!"
Strawberry had boyfriends
And all of their butts would stink
I know this because when they'd get up from chairs,
I used to smell their seats!
Vanilla had boyfriends
Who all thought they where cool with me.
"Hey, stop touching my sister, man!
I got you, bro; you don't want to fool with me!"
They all seemed to want vanilla and strawberry
But, they had to go through chocolate first!!
It was even hard for them to get married
These dudes brought their best,

I brought the worst!
Vanilla used to scratch me
And dig the skin out of her fingernails!
Strawberry used to attack me
With butcher knives,
One time she had a nail!
My sisters,
My family,
My A-listers,
Helped make a man of me.
I learned to go on dates
And sit in the backseat
If you tried to kiss my sister
You <u>will</u> smell my feet!
They've always been patient
Full of wisdom and care
They've always been loving
When others wouldn't dare.
When I call them just to say, "Hello."
They're always peaceful, always mellow.
Not as busy as fruit cup
Not as silly as jello
More reliable than whipped cream
Yeah, we were more like ice cream.
We're not really as mushy as pudding pops
Donuts or some sweet pastry tarts
No, we're ice cream.
Neopolitan to be exact.
Three flavors squeezed together in that paper box
Trying to stick to the facts
We're as tight as Fort Knox,
No other flavors went together as well as we did
Neopolitan.......the Murrell kids.

Introduction 35

"NORM"

How many of us know a woman who should have stayed in her marriage, but she became hardhearted and bitter and left before she counted up the real cost of leaving? Now she's paying for making a hasty decision about her man based upon advice taken from someone who should have never advised her. Far too often in today's society women are leaving men prematurely and making a mess of their lives as well as the man's, let alone the children.

On the other hand, there are a few women out there who should have left a long time ago. Their families and friends have watched a bright, intelligent and vibrant woman turn into a depressed, dull, frustrated and abused shell of her former self. She is dying to get out of the relationship, but doesn't have the courage. Go find that woman and tell her, "Today is the day your norm gets Elevated to 'Abundant Life'!" If you're going to call her sister, then don't let her die.

35
"NORM"
05.11.10
3:45p

Your norm isn't even warm
It's cold and askew
Indifference is like a swarm
Taking over and it didn't even ask you.
You wear silence as a badge of obedience
Even though violence isn't one of the ingredients
It's abuse in its most insidious form
Your house isn't even a home
No, it's a dorm.
Your predator issues out titles
That seems, to you, so generous
But you are cold, losing your vitals
Your weather is only in the winter months.
Everyone sees and watches this pig wear you as his pearls
It is his pleasure to wear you like a wig that has no curls
You've learned to function like a mannequin for many years
But, you better not have an unction to change a bulb or make a sandwich
You are controlled by your fears.
Unstable emotionalism has been the true man of your house
Year after year you are a remote-controlled spouse.
So now it's growing old and you are growing weary
It's time to be bold and respond to your own theory.
That theory that you spoke of before that about man
You've been leery about following that theory or to even take a stand.
How can your loved ones just sit back and watch your joy be crushed
I've seen your happiness often turned to dust.
I'm sorry for you and the way you have chosen
You need to find the Promised Land and to be your own Moses.

Don't be afraid, you've become an expert at handling fear
Don't quit searching until a new day is finally clear.
Don't let this abuse, any longer, be your normal
You don't have to be so official about it, you can be informal
Because you've devised for yourself a new life plan
You've paid your dues and deserve a better man
It's time to stop pretending that things will get better
You might need to sit down and write that letter
Now, I'm not trying to instruct you on what you should do
No, I'm merely suggesting 'it's time to really see it through'
So, I'm leaving you to your decision while these thoughts are still warm
If you don't make a decision, who does it really harm?
Only you have the power to change your norm.

Introduction 36

"Not a Victim Anymore"

This is a hard admittance. As a man, I want to hide my shame of being in relationship that made it difficult to recognize my own self in the mirror. But if I am going to be honest, I have to admit that I've been here more than once. I believe that everyone is born with a destiny and purpose to build, lift and make the world a better place. However, not everyone will discover that purpose. Some people will never find their true purpose or calling in life. They have, instead, settled for regulating everyone else's happiness in order to teach you that you are out of your league. They are determined to classify you as a victim so that you can join in their circle of misery, where they are comforted – comparing your peace with theirs through the telescope of scrutiny.

Although they will never achieve genuine peace, they are hell bent on preying upon your potential until they secure a position of permanency that affords them a steady stream of imposed power. Liberation from this type of tyranny will not only teach you valuable life lessons, but it will also bring value to your life. You will never ever answer a casting call for any one else's definition of your purpose. I offer you my congratulations.

Here, the victimization is about sex. If you've never become someone's prey, keep living. One day you may wake up and wonder, "What am I doing here!?"

36
"Not a Victim Anymore"

Ending an unbearable era in my life
Is what I'm choosing to do.
I cannot do this anymore.
It has taken all it could choose.
I've been the mat at your door.
And now, I am through.
I cannot do this anymore.
Your victimization is systematic
And you're standing on my neck, too.
Your intimidation came with a beautiful smile
With a reason, a promise and an excuse.
Then it became a threat with an irrefutable vile
You tried to hang me with a rope and a noose!
And then came the demand upon my sex.
You got what you wanted time and time again
I'm not your acquaintance; you gave me no respect
I found out, I'm not even your friend.
You are the queen of 'next'!
So, now I'm broken down with a broken back
Unspoken for and I'm always walking back.
You may no longer victimize me.
Enough is enough!!
I don't need you to patronize me
I'm not afraid of your bluff
Your effort for dominance frustrates me
It frustrates me because I let you feel I need you.
I'm embarrassed when I plead with you.
I can no longer feed you.
Leave me alone now!
Go away from me!
I am left with nothing.

You have nothing left to say to me!
This deep dark nothingness precludes me again,
Like the light of the morning, I'm loving me again
I've mourned myself far too many times
I've searched for myself far too many nights
So, I'll stay home, shut it down
And let loneliness transform me
Into the person I once loved
I'll let happiness adorn me!
Until I'm ready to face the world again
With more than just a body for someone to use
There won't be any mazes or mysteries
There won't be any clues
My life is for me to choose to offer
And so is my best essence
I've settled to lose too often
This is my resurrection
This is my best lesson!

Introduction 87

"On a Hillside"

Just take the time to reach out to someone. You may not feel that you are the person who can affect this person with your life the way that they need to be affected, but you are. They've been waiting for that special someone; but even they cannot identify a hero in a crowd. If, right now, you are thinking of someone, you are called to them. You have just identified your special someone.

The one thing the downtrodden have become experts in is watching every single person pass them by. However, you could be the one who will change their life forever in a coffee shop, while walking in the park, in a reception hall or on a quiet hillside.

37
"On a Hillside"
08.28.10

On a hillside I found your heart
Your heart was over there looking at me
When it saw me
It parted who I was
And saw the redness of my heart
You helped me peel through this madness
That was my menace.
Through the great tree in the distance,
The sun won the day over and over.
On a hillside my eyes believed
That your eyes needed
What was in the palm of my hand.
My palms bled too much as I read to you.
Your heart led me to
Become friends with you.
And then you held me up until…
On a hillside, I found your heart.
You presented your heart
With a newly found ribbon and bow
Like a present you've never given before
I parted the bow, I saw the ribbon
Looking past the box and the stuffing inside
I saw the redness of your heart.
Living inside.
Together we peeled off madness.
Together we peeled off mistrust.
Together we peeled off the day,
As it sank into the night…
On a hillside.

Introduction 38

"For Addison"

For my beautiful daughter, Addison Jamese' Murrell, I write this poem.

I remember when you were born; you look right up at me and into my eyes. You immediately grabbed hold of my finger with your whole hand and just looked at me. Nothing was lost in that moment. You knew exactly who I was and I knew your destiny would be great!

As you go about your life, Sweetheart, you will never have any question as to your father's love for you. Not only do I love you, I love you as I love myself. You are my seed. If God allows, I will be there every step of the way in your journey to becoming a woman. I know your gift to this world. I can see it in your eyes.

I want you to know that you have filled your daddy's heart with more joy than he ever thought he deserved. I've experienced joy as your father like nothing else has ever brought me. So, when you see Daddy doing wonderful, marvelous things, when you see Daddy love other people, teach other people, help other people, just remember, no one,....no one is my Addison, my sweet beautiful little girl.

My gift, my seed, my love.

38
"For Addison"

I want you to understand that
there is nothing more special to me
Than to see you prosper in life and most of all, be free.
I take it to heart when you cannot find love
I am always concerned when you're not thought of.
Without any images of honor and respect
I don't want you to cling to what you'll soon reject.
You're precious to me and all of our family
You're special to me and soon, the woman you'll be.
Take hold of this advice from someone who dearly cares
That you must choose to live your life
with giving and with prayer.
Always know that you are your greatest gift
And others may not earn the privilege to share you.
And the most important thing is this,
Don't let your uncommon nature scare you.
You were conceived in love
From your mommy and daddy
You were conceived in my heart
And you've always made me happy
Just a word to remember every day,
You are extraordinary in every way.
I love you.

Daddy

Introduction 39

"KING"

I want Black men to be encouraged to begin to fully embrace some aspect of their African American heritage and reclaim a certain level of pride they may have never known or seen in themselves or the people they see from day to day. We all need positive images that will lead to positive identities. Who we consider ourselves to be is largely determined by the influences we ingest on a daily basis. I consider myself a king although I'm also in this group of men who need daily influence in his own life.

There is no mistake about it, check your real history. In America, the Black man still doesn't have a place to derive his culture from. Almost every other nationality has access to his/her origin; and whether they think about it or not, they use the knowledge of their identity to function in everyday life. If you ask most Americans where they are from usually they can break down their bloodline into countries, nationalities, history and even tribes. When you ask most black people all we usually can say is "I'm black."

Being 'black' has not provided the necessary pride we need to sustain our dignity as a people. We cannot build only on a legacy of slavery. It is not a place for us to begin to know ourselves. The uninformed Black man goes about creating cultures based upon his current condition; his anger and resentment or small glimpses of prosperity he may have witnessed on the street or on television just so he can do what every other man has been able to do in his country – connect to a legacy or at least find an identity beyond the one that was created for them.

Even if that legacy or culture cannot make him proud, he still needs to know where he fits. If today, you identify with Christians or some other group, you still cannot ignore your natural origin – your dark skin and your kinky hair, full lips, eminent swagger or creativity. America won't let you if you tried!

Black men, take your place, in this society and in history. Without stepping onto a pedestal; simply straighten your back, open your mind and move completely forward refusing to ever look back again at what has never worked for you or your people. Find a mentor. Do those things that will first build you up as a man then turn your attention to your family. And once you are qualified, open your mouth and give life to your people. Re-evaluate all the things you swear to and against. Examine the men around you that you call your friends. Are you and your 'friends' a part of the solution or are you part of the problem? No matter your background you need to know that, in everything you do, you are leading royal people.....today. The question is, where are you leading these royal people?

So, as you choose to walk in royalty and the authority it brings, you give others – the downtrodden, the woman in despair, the children with no direction, the leaders and the hopeless, permission to do the same by your consistent example of a bonafide KING. As iron sharpens iron, I crown you once again as my brother, THE KING.

39
"KING"
2002

This cannot be a mystery.
I want to make this perfectly clear;
You have a place in history
Let me tell you the reason others fear.
And I don't want you to be ignorant.
No, I don't want you to be deceived.
For in your veins runs the blood of princes.
You bear the mark of kings.
Make no mistake about it. Whatever you believe,
Wherever you may go, I would not have you deceived.
You do not have a legacy of pimps and thieves!
You are not destined to spend one day in jail
It is not your job to manipulate and deceive.
Stop expecting black men to fail.
You are a king, with an inherited royal crest!
You are a spectacular being;
Your heritage is branded on your chest!
We are a people chosen and commissioned
To make manifest this perfect vision,
For our nation's ears stand on edge
Waiting for you to lead us closer,
Closer to making a new pledge.
A pledge that says we will no longer be of selfish indulgence
But you can look to me for fortitude and integrity;
I will use my intelligence.
This pledge is to all who have lost their way
But live to grow and fight for true freedom another day.
Together we will charter a new path
Together we will honor sacrifices past.
A King, yes, it's who you were then

And it's who you are now
No matter how much the others
Don't want you to be proud.
You can have dominion over your own domain!
No remnants of mediocrity remain
A king, yes, today.
So, take your place in history
Not another day, can this, to you, be a mystery.

Introduction 40

"Silenced"

Not many people know that I was well aware of my gift and calling as a child. I figured the only way for me to fulfill my purpose in life was to go through the church I grew up in. I did not know any better nor did I know anything different. As the people began to recognize my gifts they started to utilize them in certain areas. I was routinely viewed as the amazing newcomer who would knock the reigning placeholder out of their position and off of their fictitiously constructed pedestal by those in power. Don't get me wrong, I know they loved me. I don't even believe their actions were meant to put me in a position of sorrow or regret at all. It was just the nature of what had developed; and usually people had a life prior to this life. The problem for me was that it was my whole life! It all took me by surprise because as a child and a young man, it was where my voice was silenced.

You see, at some churches pastors could and would 'silence' you for sinning; or, in this case, what was perceived as sin. During counseling, we were encouraged to confess any sins we had committed to the pastor. I've since believed that some of the things I confessed were not sin nor were they kept completely confidential. Perhaps it was not on purpose. Perhaps it was not intended to expose you, but rather in an effort to protect or cover themselves. Nevertheless, leaders did what they thought best with the deep personal confessions they tried to keep secret. I've since learned that confession is good for the soul, but maybe not for others who don't know how to keep situations private.

Men and women of God must be spiritually mature enough not to impose any of their personal beliefs upon anyone. Just as important, their judgment should not be based on grandma's philosophy, daddy's traditions or people's prejudices, personal biases, etc.

They must use wisdom as opposed to a series of clichés and favorite scriptures that keep people in the box they've created in order to keep control over the church they feel they own.

When there are deeper confessions, a leader must be positioned to hear a heart crying, "I need to be rescued, I'm trapped, I'm being abused or I need the love of this ministry to embrace me!" It was during this time that I dealt with astronomical levels of church intimidation. Quite frankly, it was more than a kid who only wanted to please his superiors should have ever experienced. The basis of the rationale I was taught back then was that if my gift belonged to God then it belonged to the church. And, if God didn't personally reveal my gift to the leadership, then it wasn't viable or relevant.

Much to my dismay, several have suffered enormous abuses right in the church. No matter how sincere their intent, the effect has been the same. You cannot dismiss logic, experience or a person's pain away with 'he's crazy' or 'she's nuts'! My assumption is that if an angel would come to these same people and have to stand before their book of passage before they were granted permission to sing for God in churches like these, well, I guess he had better have a whiter robe, or at least some bigger wings. If this has happened to you, just know that as long as you have breath in your body, you have a voice. I offer you a license not to be silent.

40
"Silenced"
09.19.08
11:49a

The choice was made that I be silenced.
My voice was muted
With a preacher's license.
With broad intimidation
You put me on a stage.
With a destructive declaration
You made sure I was changed.
I've been silenced,
Quieted by jealousy,
Raped by envy,
Though elevated eloquently.
You could never take what was in me.
God placed a song in my heart
And a pen in my hand
And said, "Speak to the people.
Speak to me…
Make them understand.
Tell of all the injustices
Tell of all the secrets.
Go ahead, say it with substance,
Piercing like needles!
Say it, scream, yell, shout aloud!
With every outburst
Your voice I'm healing.
My son, you make me proud!
What they've done to you,
I would never do!
You are a part of me
Don't you know I've called you?"

They silenced me
And reinvented my name
But, God gave me my own song
My songs, even the angels sang.
My voice is one they learned
While I sang to my King love notes
Heaven listened
To my voice, every word,
Even when I spoke.
No one can take my worth
No one can take my blessing
Silenced on earth
But never in heaven
Now I'm giving birth,
This is my gift, Dear Lord
This is my present.

Introduction 41

"Speaking in Tongues"

To some churches and some people, speaking in tongues is a new thing. It is viewed as some sort of spiritual status symbol or level of one's perceived holiness. No one wants to be caught without that 'gift from God' that says you are so deep and so spiritually evolved it is beyond human comprehension. But it is just not that simple. The holy, tongue-talking, Bible-thumping, holy rollers of the old days were adamant about the need for it for the purpose of Salvation and that it needed to show up in church services on Sunday. Beyond that little was relayed about the Holy Ghost's place in your everyday life.

Far too many in Holiness condemned denominations that had not yet embraced the revelation of the Holy Ghost. Even more problematic was the lack of victory in the lives of those who claimed to have the Holy Ghost. What was evident was a lackluster life filled with a boatload of restrictions. We witnessed as the power of the Holy Ghost moved through services, miracles, interpretations of tongues, people receiving the Holy Ghost for the first time, communication with God and so on. But the Holy Ghost we saw in the lives of saints had weak limited benefits that only went a few steps outside of what we knew as tongues.

While a beautiful moment of when God fills Believers with His Spirit, it has been given little understanding after all these years. Although they emphasized the need for the indwelling presence and power of the Holy Ghost, there seemed to be this strong allegiance to deep personal struggle as a way of life. Consequently, they had little or no power over their finances, weight, credit the perceived enemy or even roaches! We were hard pressed to locate their power in living or experience their living or experience their love of life. It seems they were more than content to breed imitators and clone copycats – a generation who did not at all possess the power of the Holy Ghosts and who were able to both mimic and mock tongues!

You can find them nearly everywhere you go – one or two individual pretenders in the midst of authentically Spirit-filled Christians going berserk, trying to 'catch the Holy Ghost'! I've always known that you cannot 'catch' the Holy Ghost as if it was some sort of virus or an alien attack something! And it is not unusual these days to see full churches of people from the pulpit to the back door making up gibberish for the sake of status! My advice to those people is to shut it all the way down, and realize that the Holy Ghost is real, and it comes with another earthly language of His own choosing, speaking through your own mouth – one which only God imparts. Thankfully, all is not lost. There is a remnant of Believers willing to be honest with themselves as well as with God – who are not willing to pretend to have power, but who desire to filled with power of God.

41
"Speaking in Tongues"
12.08.09
11:30p

You're going to have to do better than that.
Doesn't sound like you're speaking in tongues at all
Just sounds like you are on crack!
The Word says for me to try the spirit by the spirit
Funny how, you believe no one but you can hear it.
What you're uttering is what we've called made up tongues
Even though you are trying to be exact.
The first clue was you screaming them to the top of your lungs!
Faking the Holy Ghost isn't cool, it's whack!
The Bible is clear on this, as a matter of fact, it's exact.
 "As the Spirit gave utterance they spoke with other tongues."
It's the Spirit, not you, whether it's spoken or even sung.
You are on full demonstration in the front of the whole church.
Speaking so hard and loud it looks like you need a nurse!
Why do you do it? We all know it ain't real.
Why would you fake what God hasn't healed?
As though we all needed to experience the vast revelation of your holiness
Perpetuating what has become an unholy mess
From this culture of religious wannabes, and righteous pretenders
To those who are connected to the Vine, you are the offender!
Jesus walked the earth, hung on a cross and died and sent us the Comforter
Not just for your comfort, but for you to be more than a conqueror!
Speaking in tongues, to you, is so that you will get your respect
Really receiving the Holy Ghost initially is something you will reject.
You've been taught that it's a weird prayer language or some sort of novelty.

That's why your tongues can't heal you or even bring you out of poverty!

"Gloooooooooooooooooraaaayyyy!!!!........."
"Avocado, hey,-El - dorado!"
"HOT-cheesy-enchilada!"…hey…..Yes, Lawd!
"Hey…haha-Hi-my-name-is-Rhonda!"
"E-comin-in-a-honda!"Oooooo……
"Tie-my-bow-tie!"
"Tie-it-tight!"
"Bob-bob-bob-boat-shop!"
"Eeeeeee----open-till-midnight!"
"Akuna,--Matata!"
"Iluvitwhenyoucallmebigpapa!"
"Shoop, Shoop, Shooby-doo-WAP WAP! Hey….."
"Hold-My-Toe-Higha!"
"Eat-A-Bowl-A-Soup!"
"BeYonce! Shakira!"
"Sha-na-na-na-na!"
"Hey! Hey! Hey! Goodbye!"

In short….they ain't real, baby!
No, you've been shortchanged!
Now you can stop slobbering
Get on your knees and start praying
No matter how you try to convince me it's still the same
Your church antics won't produce any change,
Clearly you think the rest of us are playing games.
Pacing, jerking lady, wearing out the church rug,
You need to sit down somewhere, do you need a hug?
Desperate, flamboyant man, drowning out the pastor,
You are called to be a son of God, stop acting like a bastard!
No, I ain't mad. Just frustrated at what we're doing in church
Maybe it's not their fault. There's so much pressure I think it hurts.
Everyone wants to be awesome and a woman or 'mand' of God
But at the risk of playing 'possum, we've placed a demand that's odd.
"How many of you are Spirit filled?' was the last word before it started.
Repentance is what we're lacking; you're speaking empty-hearted.
You're speaking an unknown language, not even from this planet.
You've convinced others that there is a new way to have it.
"We heard them speaking in our own language in which we were born."

Not some new language that has interpreters perplexed and has them torn.
Those who don't know the difference believe you are called
and are spiritually special.
Jesus is still waiting for you to be a yielded heart and a willing vessel.
So, please give up this fictitious practice
Vow to be real, not an actor, not an actress
And let God fill you for real
Your soul, He longs to really, really heal.

Introduction 42

"Sweet Mother of Mine"

It's funny...you would think that I was the most awful son growing up because we didn't seem to get along. Well, I am probably a certain kind of Mama's boy – not the kind who wanted her to take care of me, but the kind who loved and adored her presence. The bond mothers and sons share is universal.

My mom is one of a kind. She's tough, caring and diplomatic. She is the Proverbs 31:16 woman who considers a field and buys it; and out of her earnings plants a vineyard. As a child, it was her demeanor in public, at church and with extended family that I most admired. She was always proud to be Mrs. Murrell and she represented better than I've ever seen anyone! At home, we argued endlessly...seemingly more than she and my dad did! You know, the classic boy trying to grow up by asserting his authority all of the time... "Testosterone is a heck of a hormone!"

My mother is smart. Always has been. Now, in her golden years she is full of humility, grace and gratitude. And there's nothing more that she cherishes more than her children.

My mother is a stickler for grammar and correct spelling. She encourages me to be a very expressive person. Her son...is a writer. But, I'm most grateful to her for her strength. I have never known a stronger woman. Her strength is quiet, stubborn, and resilient. I've known about the heartaches she has endured; the disappointments, the disrespect and the pain. I've seen my father carry her when she couldn't walk. I've seen him care for her when she was sick countless times. I've seen her come back from a near fatal car accident a little over a year ago where she suffered a broken spine and internal injuries. Heard about the times when she screamed out in pain so loudly in the hospital people could hear her in the waiting room. My mother, a woman who was born weighing 1½ lbs. in the 1930's, survived! My mother, a woman who birthed three strong children and lost three children. I've seen her survive and survive and survive! I'm so proud of her. This one is for my one and only mother.

Love you, Mom.

42
"Sweet Mother of Mine"

My Mama is my Mama
And she's sweet as apple pie,
Ala mode.
It has been my heart's desire
For me to tell her why,
How I owe...
Her and...
Why I love her and have this gratitude
A son's love should always be of this magnitude
She's always taught me to expect the best
And to love God above all the rest
She is, to me, like rubies and far above
She is like sapphire; she is the bluest in love
I will take the times she scolded me
As proof my Mama molded me
Her resilience is as rare as volcanic afterlife
Her dreams and her body were often her sacrifice
The kind of mother who survives
The loss of three children
Is the kind of mother who deserves
The best of three more.
There is no match to her resilience,
No woman like her before.
My Mama, purely, her soul is wise.
All of the research, she defies.
As strong as an Oak tree in a winter storm
She is as comforting as a summer day and just as warm.
Your heart can confide your deepest decision
Her eyes light up when you talk
About her children
She won't have you in their lives

If you don't plan to fill them
She's often misunderstood,
But give her last? Yeah, she would.
She's sweet as apple pie…
Apple pie ala mode.

Introduction 48

"My Skin My Body"

It is funny how we live within our own bodies and live in our own skin and never truly look at ourselves with any type of admiration as to the wonder in which God has made us stewards over. The human body is truly one of God's most beautiful, complex and fascinating creations. When you can see your body as your gift only then can you really begin to respect it and present it to the world in its best light.

There are people that would have you perceive yourself as a second-class citizen simply because of your skin, skin tone or your ethnic features. Those people would have you to believe that all of your self-esteem was gifted to you by them. If they gave it to you, then they can take it back. You are beautiful, just the way you are.

God is not sitting somewhere making apologies for the flawed hue of your skin or any of your attributes for that matter. Your body is a house. Go get you some drapes, some furniture, some plumbing, some paint, a mop and a broom! Make it as amazing as intended! Celebrate life! Celebrate your skin!

I feel everyone should write a poem about their body in the affirmative. I was actually asked to write this poem after a modeling photo shoot in which I was celebrating my brown-skin and my African/Native American features in a book of art. Since I already had a healthy self image, this served as confirmation of the way I saw myself – as a gift.

43
"My Skin My Body"

My skin, my body
How it changes with time and in the light
Warm and strong,
Like Columbia's mahogany coffee beans
Dark like Morocco
Void of flaws or need of correction.
My aura, my essence,
My convictions and beliefs
Deepen the dark recesses of my skin.
My hands are black
My chest is hard
And I can feel the world
Through my body's art.
I trust the skin
I live within.
Course, thick black hair ripples
Across the expanse of my body
In harmony to the music
Of my masculine structure
Dancing rhythmically
To an African beat
Living physically
In the African heat
My skin, my body…
How it changes with time and in the light.

Introduction 44

"The Conscious Subconscious"

There are some things in life we can plead the fifth on...then again; there are times we must simply confess our guilt. One of which is when that all-too-familiar voice within us is commenting, correcting and calling us to the examining room to look at the complete picture – to consider the ramifications and potential consequences of what we're about to do. That life changing next step into the dumb and stupid abyss of playing ignorant and becoming deaf to the warnings shouted or horns blown to either cause us to stop immediately turn and run or move forward fearlessly.

It is with us at every turn – existing in every nook and cranny of our being. It is more real than we'd care to admit; the undeniable, immutable presence of the conscious subconscious.

44
"The Conscious Subconscious"
Fall 2009

You may pretend
To be pretending,
But in the end
You're only defending
A reality that isn't even yours.
So, when I lend you
My mending
You may offend me
With what you're pretending
And hurt me with that even more.
I'm not trying to be condescending
But, the thing you've been sending
Really needs an ending
Before you're befriending
Those whom you say you adore!
Your Conscious Subconscious
Knows what I'm talking about
And it really knows that I'm right.
In this, you need to have no doubt
Resolved to what you're about
And change your end inevitably in sight.
So if you can handle this citation
I will promise to be patient
Until you feel the sensation
To make a proclamation
To change the way you remain a friend.
So, check your foundation
At what has captured your fascination,
And removed your adaptation.
You need a strong variation

Of your original declaration
Make a deeper alteration
So that we both can find a peaceful end.
You can go focus your tokens
On your love 'hocus pocus'.
Maybe you will change your focus
You will see what finally broke us.
It ate through us like a locust .
Yes, it was your past that did choke us.
The conscious subconscious is full of revelations
No room for your cunning and lofty innovations
So, make this your shameful and naked coronation
This is the last time I make this confrontation.
The End.

Introduction 45

"The Empire"

This place that exists so vividly within my imagination is a place that I've subliminally dreamed of since I was a child. So when I finally allowed myself to write it down, it was as familiar to me as if describing my childhood home.

In my mind and heart, I have lived this scenario in many ways. Take a walk with the royal family and me as we gracefully embark upon the saga of the epic account of this legendary name – Murrell.

In 'The Empire' my family is considered royalty. We live there with all of our imperfections, yet filled with love for one another.

Parents have to be aware of their affect on their children. Children will treat the world they way they learned to treat each other because of their parents' example. I love my family. You may love your family just the same. If you didn't have the luxury of this type of family, you can borrow mine. Welcome to THE EMPIRE.

45
"The Empire"

Palaces of ivory and jade, marble and onyx
Gemstones upon a black sandy shore
I watch as my father, the Emperor
In all of his eminent glory, strolls down
A massive set of ivory stairs unto his black sanded beach
Dressed from head to toe in his royal crown, kingly attire
And ten foot heavily embroidered robe
That would billow down every step behind him.
My father sees me and smiles.
He beckons for me to join him.
I am dressed in a sort of half robe with sleeves with fur cuffs,
Pants made of the riches cowhide and kingly sandals
My crown is tilted to the side...
We walk along the beach
As we walk, we survey the land across the sea,
The castles and villas on the hill, and the town below the distant hill.
It is the perfect day.
My dad, the Emperor.
Me, the Prince.
Swan perform a synchronized ballet across the waters
Our dog runs down the stairs to join us.
The only thing more beautiful than the glistening shores
Are the glistening stones in our crowns
It is Monday and a day before New Year's Day
And the castle is lit up with lights, decorations and anticipation
It is also the king's birthday!
The entire kingdom is preparing to celebrate
Not only the king's birthday, but to celebrate his greatest love,
My mother, the queen.
She is waiting in the vast beach house I see in the distance
She is dressed in white, my sisters are in white

White sheer curtains are blowing outward
Welcoming the sea to come in
It's a good day and all is well.
Pigs are roasting and feasts are being prepared
Servants are bringing in exotic fruits and imported oils
The air is filled with fresh cut flowers
Healing plants and fresh water
The night's sky will be filled with fireworks
We are joining together for prayer before the rest of the family arrives.
Just as the prayer ends I hear the bells ring out at the castle
The family has arrived……
WELCOME TO THE EMPIRE!!!

Introduction 46

"The Father's Love"

Whether or not you consider yourself religious, more than likely you are aware of a Being or God that you recognize as the creator of all that exists in your world. For clarification, He would be considered your Father. Your Father's love is unconditional and far exceeds anything you've ever experienced. My heavenly Father is the source of all the love I've come to understand in my life. He is not the author of any confusion in my life, but He desires that I align my will with His. His will is all about me receiving more love.

I am not confused about plight and struggle in the world and in my life. I am grateful for His direction through His Word. When you are raised without any knowledge of the Word you may have to struggle to understand why so many things happen in the world. Even with the knowledge of the Word, it can be a process in acceptance, humility and grace. This is all about understanding your position in the world and in your life at the same time understanding who God is.

Many go through their lives with the belief that He is the "Ultimate Santa Claus" or some Big Genie that needs to grant wishes in order to have relevance. While others believe His only goal is to make people's life miserable, I come to tell you that our God is love.

"For God so loved the world that He gave His only begotten Son, that whosoever believeth in Him should not perish, but have everlasting life." John 3:16

"Herein is love, not that we loved God, but that He loved us, and sent His Son to be the propitiation for our sins. Beloved, if God so loved us, we ought also to love one another."   1 John 4:10-11

46
"The Father's Love"
April 2001

Broad strokes on an artist's canvas
Sunsets on rural plains
Black silver dances in my eyes
As the clouds bring torrential rains
Now, comes the eerie thunder
And dense moments of silence
As I listen it makes me wonder
If God is prone to violence.
Like a Denver morning breeze
Charged with a day's purpose,
Fluid with an anticipating ease,
As nature's servant.
The Father loves…
Like time removed from its axis
Moments purposed in nurturing and growth
Is a lifetime of healing to His children
From the gentle winds the Father brings them hope
Fields of golden wheat sway in rhythm
Flocks of fowl design patterns with them
On an unmitigated blue hued canvas
The feet of his most precious ones toil
Churning the earth's soil
Until we have all been moved …forward
From the Father's love

Introduction 47

"The Huddle"

Many of us spend our entire lives in the huddle – in trenches, churches or institutions that are designed to build life as well as to give life to those who are in need of our gifts. They are camouflaged in our jobs, our careers, our callings and even our ministries. In this poem, I refer to the church as the huddle. The most powerful people of the world assemble in churches to benefit from like spirits and be in the presence of God. As such, it is potentially the most powerful place on earth. This particular huddle does not refer to Muslims, Buddhists or worshippers of other gods. It is a specific reference to the place Christians gather together for strength, understanding and clarity for our lives outside of the huddle.

In football, team players come together for understanding, instruction and unity before facing their opposition. They remain until they have achieved a desired cohesiveness from which they can then walk away with one goal and enter the battle. The huddle has been described as 'to crowd together', a 'tight circle formed in which to strategize against an opponent' or a cluster. This writing is my homage to my belief in….the huddle.

47
"The Huddle"

The wind, the water, the waves, the ocean
The moving, the rocking, the twisting, the motion
The bustling, the hammering, the blistering, the swell
To the rumbling, the tussling, the fight, the smell
The breaking, the melting, the bruising, the choke
The insults, the cursing, the belittling, the smoke
All a part of our lives and the emanate struggle
To become one with each other and enter the huddle
The huddle, a place of refuge and fellowship
My brother, my sister, it's ok to settle in
To the wind, the water, the waves, the ocean
The moving, the rocking, the twisting, the motion
The rivers that swirl, filter and dive
Comes back and floods in to make you feel alive.
Bring me, sing me, ring me asleep,
Sing me, king me, stay with me into the deep
There is purpose here
There is life forever
I bring my service here
I bring my life's endeavor
So that many things may become real,
Become better, come clear.
All that you are and all that I truly am
Can become holy, can become reality
In the presence of the King, we are royalty
There is life.......in the huddle.
There is love......in the huddle.
There is forgiveness....in the huddle.
There is peace......in the huddle.
There is strength....in the huddle.
There are others who think just like you, like me.....in....the huddle.

Introduction 48

"The Sacrifice"

This writing pleased me to complete. It is the final proof that I'm on the way out of a mentality that had me making poor decisions on a regular basis. Thankfully, very few of those decisions were major. I'm a man who takes his time and carefully weighs his options. But, there were times when I made decisions out of my own dysfunction and need. I couldn't really tell you how I got to that point, but once it happened, I was forced to examine myself so that I would never have to learn life's lessons in that same manner. By the way, men fail in relationships too.

48
"The Sacrifice"
01.21.06
10:30p

All too often
I sacrifice at the wheel
All too familiar
I identify that same appeal
That there have been too many instances,
Too many circumstances,
Too many coincidences,
Too many second chances.
All too often
I sacrifice at the wheel
You want my birthright and power
You want to take me from the living room
To the showers.
All too familiar
Is this pain in my vision
It is my decision,
I give permission to imprison!
Why can't you support
What God has predestined?
Your plan is abort
Anything that isn't your blessing!
I sacrificed and now I repent,
Because what I thought was love
Has now got me bent!
Take back this sacrifice
And give me back my soul
I'm giving you free advice
It was never yours to hold.
Let go.

Introduction 49

"You Took My Choice Away"

The subject of exposing male sexual abuse may be too difficult for most male victims to allow themselves to speak about. Most people believe that this particular population of survivors is very small because of the stigma placed upon men and boys who have been abused. Actually, nothing could be further from the truth. It is my understanding that with anything, 'when the men begin to heal, we all heal.'

While working in several treatment centers, group homes and with youth in general, I found that a vast majority of young men and boys have been sexually abused as children. About half of them don't even believe it was sexual abuse at all. Many were taught they were only little men, 'playas', and were congratulated from time to time as they relayed stories of babysitters, caregivers or teachers fondling or exposing themselves to them. Thus never giving the child a voice to say, "Please, someone! I need an adult to rescue me!" I often say, if he lost his virginity at age 8 from a girl who was 18, why was she interested in an 8 year old? Now, take that same scenario and reverse the sexes....... I'll wait...... Now, do you see what I mean? This has got to end! It is the lie that keeps it going.

I am admitting to you I am a victim as well. I've kept this a secret for most of my life only because, like every man, I don't want to be placed in an unfair category and be judged in everything I do. I fully realize that I did not deserve, coerce, entice, induce or seduce any of the decisions made by my adult perpetrator. . Still, I tried, with all of my might, to remain a healthy, lovable, sweet and well-rounded kid. The abuse in my life was so severe that it filtered over into every other aspect of my life; and I might add, without my permission. I understand the grip, the mental leech, the stain and relentless pain a man has to live with while doing his best to learn to be a man. I am happy to say that I have survived, and am now strong enough to, for the first time, break my silence about one of my greatest battles.

This is about one man's journey from being a severely sexually abused child to that of a successful and productive member of society. It left deep scars within me, but it also taught me about the king that lived inside the kid, the man inside the boy; even in the worst times. I wrote this poem addressing the person who did this to me as a verbal confrontation. If you are like this me, I hope this gives you the courage to tell someone, anyone that you trust so that you will begin to heal as I did. Even as a grown man you need to heal and protect the wounded little boy that still lives inside.

49
"You Took My Choice Away"
Sunday 12.28.08
3:39 p

There I was, clean and ripe for picking.
I was so young and innocent
Seemed the clock, for me, had not begun ticking
My life was focused away from any norm you knew
Me, like a lost penny
Unwanted, yet all shiny and new.
Taking advantage may not be what you thought
But you took your chances
What was more important was not getting caught
From the first day of your manipulation
To the last day of our confrontation
From the many years I was hampered
Still picking up the pieces
The tears linger many years afterward
And yet, the anger never ceases.
This stain is like a burgundy growth on my face
This pain is still strong because of the disgrace.
Everyone tells me to let go of the shame
These same people, to others, whispered my name.
They've whispered speculations and judgments.
As if I didn't know or hear them
It doesn't help me grow, it really doesn't,
All they want me to do is to clear them.
Most like me compare themselves,
In the Bible, to Job
I compare myself to Lazarus
Or Joseph with the colorful robe
I'm fighting devours everyday
My manhood grows sour in the wake

You took my choice from me
I'm not what I used to be
In turn you took my voice from me
And left me with this hidden thing.
Never mind what has happened to you as a result
This ain't about you
I was a child, you were an adult
Who will help me with my broken wings?
Who wants to see me fly?
I'm like a wounded duckling
Can't you hear me cry?
I'm shouting, I'm screaming...
Enough is enough!
Spent so many years dreaming.
I am the toughest of the tough!
Can't give in to it, no, I can't quit!
This isn't my life
No matter how it persists!
It is evil no doubt
It intends to never let me out
You took my choice away
Never allowing me a real childhood
You cut me down like a desert tree
Using me for firewood
Left to burn me out
Even though I was a kid
You tried to turn me out!
No matter what I did.
You said you loved me
And you would always wish me well,
Your love was so ugly
You didn't even want it for yourself.
Now that the boy is grown
And I finally get to choose,
My choice is now my own
And I'm determined not to lose!
Found out God had already chosen me
Before He made this earth
He knew about this moment for me
Before the day of my birth.
So even though it was stolen from me
It's not gone forever.

God saw me and **He** promised me
That He would make it better.
What you did is not forgotten.
But it is forgiven,
Though the stench is rotten.
And it feels like a prison
My voice has returned!
And so has my choice.
No longer burned,
Now with a deeper voice.

Introduction 50

"The Inmate"

I cannot believe what I'm about to write. There are some of you that know me who will have a hard time believing what I'm about to write as well. Well, here is my truth. In August, 2012, I was wrongly convicted of a charge of contempt, and was ordered to serve six months in the county jail. As long as I live I may never forget the moment when the judge's gavel came down, and the order was final.

I felt nothing in my life had prepared me for this travesty! I was literally in shock! I didn't know whether to throw up, pass out or simply die as they handcuffed me while standing right there in front of the judge and a courtroom full of people. Standing there in my blazer, dress shirt, loafers and khaki pants. It was, to say the least, wrong and unfair because I was never given the opportunity to plead my own case.

My first thought was, "God!! I know You aren't going to do this to me! I can't believe You think that I can take this on top of everything else!" But before He could reply I reasoned, I am the same James Murrell that I know You love! I have never purposely harmed anyone. I am a poor liar, who loves honesty and thrives on the truth. I couldn't steal even if I tried. I began to remember all of the other hard things He's brought me through. As I sat in the jury box waiting to be taken away by law enforcement, I tried really hard not to panic. I was focused on breathing.

I honestly could not make sense of the fact that this was actually happening... What possible purpose could this serve? Why would anyone want to keep me away from my own daughter for six months!?? Needless to say, I felt completely rejected. I thought God was tired of me, and this was His way of saying that He had finally had enough of me. But God showed His hand mighty! What happened in this process was nothing short of a MIRACLE!!! Talk about a 'ram in the bush'! I was about to experience another level of His grace! So of all the titles I have been blessed to have, I never thought I'd ever be called……..the inmate.

50
"The Inmate"
08.12

They put that orange uniform in a bag for me
They put two pairs of orange socks in a bag for me
They put those orange boxers, sheets and blanket
In a mesh laundry bag just for me
I walk through the corridor of one's destiny
I carried that cold plastic mattress over my shoulder in one hand
A bag of community clothing in the other.
I walked down the hallway with the other men who were also convicted
This long, wide and deep highway designed for shaming me
Walking in those ill-fitting sandals that have been on countless men's feet
In the state of shock, not believing this was me.
Even the most stable, confident and accomplished man
Would begin to question his worth
Leading to a dwelling of obscurity – the Pods
Beyond a sea of orange uniforms one can't help
But notice the intentional Art-Deco design
Of the entire space. Why is that?
What was the designer's purpose?
Was it to impress designing inmates?
Or was it to impress money holders with a stake in the
Demise of the men who would come here?
Was it to speak of the control and rule of men's lives as an ultimate power?
Daily, we were treated as men who had no rights.
Is that possible? Are there men born with no rights?
This is just the beginning of my tale as… the inmate.
I never thought there would be anyone in my life who wanted to hate me so.

What had I done? Had I attacked someone? Stolen from someone? Been unfair to someone? Had I purposely cheated someone? Had I beaten someone?
Had I murdered someone? Had I done anything to any soul on this earth to belong here?
Taken to a cell and slammed the door.
I turned around and looked out the glass.
Trying to grasp the fact that someone felt I needed to be jailed.
I kept thinking about my daughter……
I kept thinking that she needed me and that I didn't have time to be in here.
What was the plan and why did someone want me out of the way?
I thought of my parents and my sisters seeing me in that orange outfit
Sad and imprisoned;
Alone and forsaken.
I was sentenced to six months by a woman.
God will always have the last say!
I endured the worst food I have ever tasted in life
I witnessed fights, liquor being made in toilets
I witnessed men making threats, perversions and mental illness.
I was offered drugs, sex and all the spoils the damned had to offer.
My conversations with God became more frequent and more intense.
I cried. I begged. I pleaded. Then I rested!
In 9days God would minister to me
In a place where I could hear this kind of message
In 9 days God would speak through me
To even those men who were once His vessels
In 9 days I would face my strengths and weaknesses
In 9 days ….while I was sentenced to 6 months……
On the 10th day I saw a miracle.
Against all odds, I went home!
I've earned the right to make this proclamation,
This is the end of MY ALIEN NATION!

Made in the USA
Monee, IL
16 January 2022